D1602385

Modern Architecture in an Oxford College

Frontispiece: An air view of the college taken c.2000, with the garden in the foreground. The older buildings are to the left, the North Quadrangle, the Sir Thomas White Building, and the Garden Quadrangle to the right (Chris Andrews)

Modern Architecture in an Oxford College

St John's College 1945–2005

Geoffrey Tyack

OXFORD
UNIVERSITY PRESS

OXFORD

UNIVERSITY PRESS

Great Clarendon Street, Oxford OX2 6DP

Oxford University Press is a department of the University of Oxford.
It furthers the University's objective of excellence in research, scholarship,
and education by publishing worldwide in

Oxford New York

Auckland Cape Town Dar es Salaam Hong Kong Karachi
Kuala Lumpur Madrid Melbourne Mexico City Nairobi
New Delhi Shanghai Taipei Toronto

With offices in

Argentina Austria Brazil Chile Czech Republic France Greece
Guatemala Hungary Italy Japan Poland Portugal Singapore
South Korea Switzerland Thailand Turkey Ukraine Vietnam

Oxford is a registered trade mark of Oxford University Press
in the UK and certain other countries

Published in the United States
by Oxford University Press Inc., New York

British Library Cataloguing in Publication Data

Data available

Library of Congress Cataloging in Publication Data

Data available

Printed in Italy by Legoprint s.p.a

ISBN 0–19–927162–3   978–0–19–927162–7

10 9 8 7 6 5 4 3 2 1

Preface and Acknowledgements

The character of most institutions of higher education in the English-speaking world is inseparable from their buildings. What would the University of Virginia be without Thomas Jefferson's classical campus, or the University of London without Charles Holden's monumental Senate House looming over Russell Square? This is especially true of Oxford and Cambridge, where the buildings reflect and embody both the antiquity of the two universities and their fragmented collegiate organization. Oxford and Cambridge colleges were, and to some extent still are, secular monasteries with communities of teachers and students working and even living in the same place: something that sets them apart from the equally ancient universities of Continental Europe, cut off by Napoleonic reorganization from their medieval roots. But unlike monasteries, where life still proceeds according to rules laid down in the Middle Ages, the colleges of Oxford and Cambridge, beneath the appearance of unchanging continuity assiduously celebrated in myth and ritual, have changed profoundly over the past sixty years. These changes are also reflected in their buildings, and it is a single Oxford college's architectural response to change that is the subject of this book.

Few subjects are more liable to prejudice and misunderstanding than modern architecture. Perhaps this is because architecture is a public art, about which everyone rightly feels entitled to an opinion. Unfortunately these opinions are not always well-informed. For many people, the flat statement 'I don't like it' is enough to condemn a building, and, at least until recently, writers on contemporary architecture were not very successful in training public taste. This may now be changing. We live in an age of consumer choice and relativistic values, in aesthetics as well as in ethics and morals. We are perhaps less inclined than we once were to rush to judgement, more open to appreciating variety, more interested in understanding buildings within their historical and intellectual context. Modernism itself has now become a historic style, revived with great skill and imagination by some of the best contemporary architects. Even the buildings of the 1950s and 1960s—long the subject of unquestioning dismissal by cultural pundits and the public at large—are far enough removed from us in time to make it possible to reassess them in a dispassionate manner. And if we understand these buildings properly we will be in a much better position to understand the often highly original and enjoyable architecture of the last thirty years.

Since the end of the Second World War St John's College has built up a record second to none in the two ancient universities as a patron of good modern architecture (I use the word 'modern' in the sense 'of the present day', as opposed to 'modernist', which I take to mean the avowedly innovative style of architecture that evolved before and just after the First World War in Europe and the United States and became the *lingua franca* throughout the world in the second half of the twentieth century). Now, as the college approaches its 450th anniversary, and contemplates another large new building project, is a good time to review the architectural achievements of the last sixty years and to attempt to relate them to its overall development during that period. During the first 400 years of its existence the college commissioned only one building of more than local architectural interest: the Canterbury Quadrangle, built in 1631–5. In the second half of of the twentieth century it has commissioned three: the Beehive of the 1950s, the Sir Thomas White Building of the 1970s, and the Garden Quadrangle of the 1990s. An understanding of their history throws light not only on the development of St John's but also on the history of recent university architecture in general: a subject of absorbing interest and importance at a time when the future of British universities, including Oxford, is a subject of public concern and debate. It is with this wider aim in mind that this book has been written.

It would have been impossible to write this book without the active cooperation of several people. Sir Howard Colvin, the doyen of English architectural historians, has been unfailingly helpful throughout the project and has read and commented on the whole manuscript. The idea of writing a book on the modern buildings of the college was conceived by the Bursar, Anthony Boyce, and he has generously placed files, drawings, and other material at my disposal as well as answering my questions about the most recent buildings and about current architectural projects. The archivist, Michael Riordan, has gone well beyond the call of duty in tracking down dusty architectural drawings as well as other material in the Muniment Room. Others who have helped by supplying information or reading parts of the manuscript include Sir Philip Dowson, Sir Richard MacCormac, Nigel Hiscock, Harry Kidd, Ross McKibbin, Matthew Nicholls, Keith Pearce, George Richardson, Tom Sherwood, and William Whyte. Anne Ashby, Paul Cleal, Bernard Dod, and Sandra Raphael at the Oxford University Press have supported this project with exemplary enthusiasm and attention to detail. I am also grateful to Boyd Hilton for showing me Richard MacCormac's Blue Boar Court at Trinity College, Cambridge; to Alan Powers for providing information about his father Michael Powers; to Lloyd Stratton and Lynn Cooper for giving me access to the records of the Architects' Co-Partnership; and to Juliet Walshe of Arup Associates, Richard Robinson of MacCormac Jamieson and Pritchard, and Chris Andrews for supplying photographs.

Oxford, February 2005

Contents

List of Illustrations

Abbreviations

ACP	Architects' Co-Partnership
SJCA, ADM I.A.	St John's College Archives, Governing Body Minutes
SJCA, Mun. lxxxi	St John's College Archives, papers on the college buildings
UGC	University Grants Committee

1 The Last Enchantments of the Neo-Georgian: the Dolphin Quadrangle

Throughout the first half of the twentieth century the new architecture of St John's College proclaimed the undemanding virtues of continuity and respect for the past. Founded in 1555 by Sir Thomas White, a merchant tailor from London, the college had taken over the site and buildings of an earlier foundation: the former St Bernard's College, established by Archbishop Henry Chichele for Cistercian monks in 1437.[1] For the next ninety years it did not expand beyond the boundaries of the institution it superseded, apart from relatively small extensions to the east (the Old Library) and the north (the kitchen and Cook's Building in the present North Quadrangle). Thanks to the munificence of Archbishop William Laud, a second, architecturally much more ambitious set of buildings—the Canterbury Quadrangle—was added to the east of the Front Quadrangle in 1631–5, with an east façade overlooking the Grove or Garden. The Canterbury Quadrangle immediately became the architectural showpiece of the St John's, epitomizing its strongly royalist and conservative character, and its richly detailed stone façades became the subject of countless drawings, paintings, engravings, and, eventually, photographs.

Subsequent additions and extensions to the college were incremental and, at first, unambitious (see Fig. 1). A Senior Common Room went up to the north of the Chapel in 1673–6 and a new residential block (the Holmes Building) to the south of the Canterbury Quadrangle in 1795. The formal gardens shown in early bird's-eye views succumbed to lawns and landscaping in 1772–8. But, apart from the internal remodelling of the Hall in 1729–30, the replacement of mullioned by sash windows in the Front Quadrangle in about 1740, and the unfortunate internal reconstruction of the Chapel by Edward Blore in 1843–4, in the mid-nineteenth century the college's buildings still looked much as they had done in the time of Charles I and Archbishop Laud.

Like all Oxford colleges except All Souls—which had no undergraduates—St John's grew in the last quarter of the nineteenth century. Before then it was an

---

[1] For the pre-twentieth-century history of the college and its buildings, see H. M. Colvin, 'The Building of St Bernard's College', *Oxoniensia* xxiv (1959), pp. 37–44; W. H. Stevenson and H. E. Salter, *The Early History of St John's College* (Oxford 1939); W. C. Costin, *The History of St John's College, Oxford 1598–1860* (Oxford 1958); and H. M. Colvin, *The Canterbury Quadrangle* (Oxford 1988). There are briefer accounts by A. Oswald in *Country Life* (2, 9 November 1929), pp. 606–14, in the Royal Commission on Historic Monuments, *City of Oxford* (1939), in H. E. Salter and M. D. Lobel, *Victoria County History of Oxfordshire* iii (1954), pp. 251–64, and in G. Tyack, *St John's College: a Short History and Guide* (Oxford 2000).

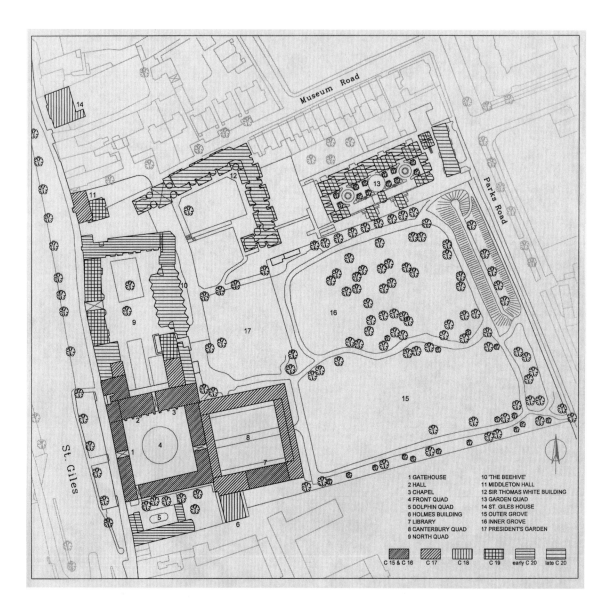

1 GATEHOUSE
2 HALL
3 CHAPEL
4 FRONT QUAD
5 DOLPHIN QUAD
6 HOLMES BUILDING
7 LIBRARY
8 CANTERBURY QUAD
9 NORTH QUAD

10 'THE BEEHIVE'
11 MIDDLETON HALL
12 SIR THOMAS WHITE BUILDING
13 GARDEN QUAD
14 ST. GILES HOUSE
15 OUTER GROVE
16 INNER GROVE
17 PRESIDENT'S GARDEN

C 15 & C 16   C 17   C 18   C 19   early C 20   late C 20

1 Ground plan of the college

overwhelmingly clerical society strongly resistant to change. But in 1861 it was forced by a government Order in Council to open up its fellowships and scholarships to competition; twenty years later, in 1881, it passed new Statutes which allowed fellows to marry and insisted that most of them taught undergraduates. With the number of students about to double (to about 180) over the next forty years, plans were drawn up in 1879 by the younger George Gilbert Scott—son of the architect of the Martyrs' Memorial and much else—for a large expansion to the north of the Cook's Building and Senior Common Room. The ground on the St Giles front was occupied by a motley collection of houses and outbuildings, and beyond the Senior Common Room was a stable block for the President's horses and carriage, built to the designs of the London architect Thomas Hardwick in

1811.[2] In Scott's first plans a new hall would have loomed over a small and dark quadrangle to the north of the existing Hall, which would have been relegated to a twilight existence, probably as a lecture room;[3] a second and more spacious residential quadrangle would have occupied the ground to the north. It would probably have been sufficient to satisfy the college's accommodation needs down to the middle of the twentieth century, but the plans were too ambitious for a college suffering, like many others, from the results of an agricultural depression, and Scott was then asked to produce a second, cheaper, design in which the new hall would be omitted.

Only part of Scott's second scheme was carried out: the western range or New Building (staircases 12–15), flanking St Giles. It was built in two stages, in 1880–2 and 1899–1900, the second stage being entrusted after Scott's death to E. P. Warren, the architect brother of the then President of Magdalen College. Scott's first design had been in the eclectic neo-Jacobean style made fashionable in Oxford by Thomas Graham Jackson. But the college preferred what it called the 'medieval' style, and the building that now occupies the western side of the North Quadrangle has Tudor Gothic detailing with no traces of Jacksonian eclecticism. Built of an ochre limestone from Taynton and Milton in the Oxfordshire Cotswolds, it provided accommodation for twenty students in spacious sets of rooms—the normal unit of student accommodation in Oxford down to the Second World War—on either side of an imposing central gate tower (Fig. 2). The rest of the quadrangle was developed piecemeal during the twentieth century.[4] In 1909–11 a new range of rooms—the Rawlinson Building (staircases 16–18)—was built along the north side to the designs of N. W. Harrison, a local architect who became surveyor to the college's North Oxford estate in 1903.[5] He too chose the Tudor Gothic style, and his carefully detailed range of light-coloured Ancaster stone buildings, with roofs of Collyweston slates, provides a pleasing termination to the view north from the entrance to the quadrangle.[6] More domestic in character than Scott's building to the west, it served its purpose well, supplying spacious, comfortable and well-detailed two-roomed sets for eighteen undergraduates. In 1933 it was extended to the east and south (staircase 19), to the designs of Edward Maufe, who departed little from the older architect's designs (Fig. 3).

Maufe was the dominant figure in the architectural history of St John's in the mid-twentieth century (Fig. 4). The son of Henry Muff, a Leeds industrialist who married a niece of the manufacturer Titus Salt and corresponded with John

[2] H. M. Colvin, *A Biographical Dictionary of British Architects 1600–1840*, 3rd edn (New Haven and London 1995), p. 460.

[3] They are discussed and illustrated in H. M. Colvin, *Unbuilt Oxford* (New Haven and London 1983), pp. 180–2.

[4] Its appearance in 1923 is shown in a drawing by E. H. New in E. G. Withypool, *The New Loggan Guide to Oxford Colleges* (Oxford, 1932), p. 41; see Fig. 2.

[5] T. Hinchcliffe, *North Oxford* (New Haven and London 1992), p. 86. He was responsible for the building of Bainton Road, and there are houses by him in Charlbury Rd, Chadlington Rd, and elsewhere on the estate.

[6] W. A. Arkell, *Oxford Stone* (1947), p. 104.

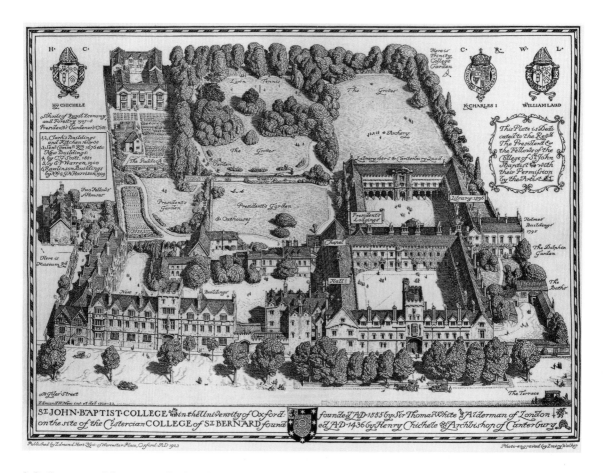

The following text appears within the illustration:

H C
Hd CHICHELE

School of Rural Economy
and Forestry 1907-8
President's Gardener's Cott.
1,2, Clark's Buildings
and Kitchen 1613-36
3. Sen'. Comm'. R'". 1676 etc.
New buildings:
4. by G.G. Scott, 1881
5. by G.F. Warren, 1900
6. Rawlinson Buildings
by N° 6 G.A. Harrison 1909

Lawn Tennis
The Groves
Hall Archery

Two Fellows'
Houses

The Paddock
The Groves
Rock Garden

President's
Garden
President's Garden
& Outhouses

Library 1601-3 & Canterbury Quad.

Here is
Trinity
College
Garden

C R W L
K. CHARLES I   WILLIAM LAUD

This Plate is Dedi-
cated to the Revd
The President &
the Fellows of the
College of St John
Baptist with
their Permission
by the Artist

Library 1596

Here is
Museum Rd.

New Buildings

President's
Lodgings

Chapel

Hall

Holmes'
Buildings
1795
The Dolphin
Garden

The
Baths

St Giles Street
Edmund H. New inv. et del 1910-23.

The Terrace

ST. JOHN·BAPTIST·COLLEGE in the University of Oxford: founded A.D. 1555 by Sir Thomas White, Alderman of London
on the site of the Cistercian COLLEGE of St BERNARD founded A.D. 1436 by Henry Chichele, Archbishop of Canterbury

Published by Edmund Hort New of Worcester Place, Oxford A.D 1923   Photo-engraved by Emery Walker

2 Bird's-eye view of the college from the west from E. H. New's 'New Loggan' views of Oxford colleges (1923). The older part of the college is to the right, with the site of the former Dolphin Inn on the extreme right. The North Quadrangle is to the left, with the President's garden behind and the Department of Rural Economy at the top left-hand corner (Bodleian Library, University of Oxford, G. A. Oxon. a. 33, f. 33 recto)

Ruskin, he spent some of his childhood in one of the shrines of the English Arts and Crafts movement: Red House at Bexleyheath in Kent, designed by Philip Webb for William Morris in 1859 and leased by Maufe's parents.[7] He received an architectural training in the office of W. A. Pite, the architect of King's College Hospital in south London, but in 1904–8, before completing his pupillage, he spent four years as an undergraduate at St John's reading Greats (classics, ancient history, and philosophy), after which he completed his training at the Architectural Association in London. In the inter-war years he established a successful practice, largely made up of country houses, churches, and banks, and in 1925 he won a prize for furniture at the Paris Exhibition, where the Art Deco style was launched.[8] At Yaffle Hill (1930), a large villa near Poole in Dorset, he applied Art Deco detailing to a house laid out on the 'butterfly' plan popular in the early years of the century.[9] But he received widespread acclaim only when he won the competition for the new Guildford Cathedral in 1932, and it is this noble Gothic building,

[7] *Dictionary of National Biography 1971–81*, pp. 559-60. He changed his name to Maufe by deed-poll in 1909. See also A. and V. Sillery, *St John's College Biographical Register 1919–1975* (Oxford, 1978), p. 27.
[8] It was included in the 'Art Deco' exhibition at the Victoria and Albert Museum in 2002–3.
[9] J. Newman and N. Pevsner, *The Buildings of England: Dorset* (Harmondsworth, 1972) p. 115; David Dean, *The Thirties: Recalling the English Architectural Scene* (London, 1983), pl. 1.

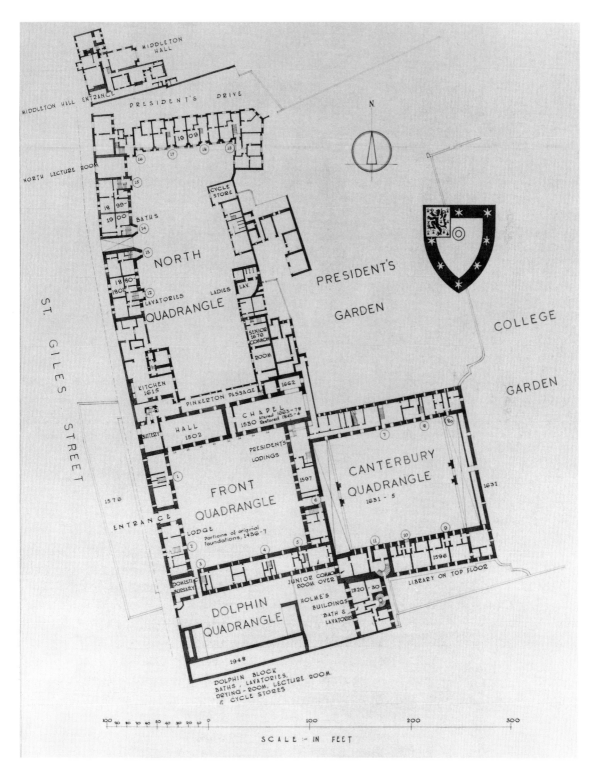

3 Plan of the college, *c.*1955, showing the staircase numbers and the dates of different parts of the buildings

4 Sir Edward Maufe (second from the left) with the President, W. C. Costin (centre right), the Bishop of Winchester (far right), and the sculptor Alan Collins (left), who carved the figures of Archbishop Chichele and Sir Thomas White over the gateway, donated by Maufe in 1961

completed in 1961, with its spacious white interior of almost Cistercian plainness, which constitutes his chief claim to fame. Like many of his English contemporaries, he was deeply influenced by Arts and Crafts ideas and shunned the innovations of the Modern movement as interpreted by Gropius, Mies van der Rohe, Le Corbusier, and their followers. Yet he admired contemporary Scandinavian architecture and design and endeavoured to express the spirit of the age in his architecture, taking 'a middle course of well-mannered modernity', in the tactful words of his biographer, 'without the grammar of classicism'.[10]

Maufe's first work at St John's took the form of memorial slabs to his former tutor Sidney Ball (d.1918) in the Canterbury Quadrangle and to Henry Jardine Bidder (d. 1923) on the wall of the rock garden that Bidder had created.[11] He later carried out several minor projects for the college: a wrought-iron gate to the President's garden (1923); a new layout of lawns and flagstones in the Canterbury Quadrangle (1935);[12] a remodelling of the smoking room of the Senior Common Room (1936);[13] the opening up of the post-Restoration Baylie Chapel to the main part of the Chapel (also 1936); and a semi-detached pair of houses for married tutors at the western end of Museum Road (1938). He also donated the statue— by Eric Gill—of St John the Baptist which looks down from the gate tower into the Front Quadrangle. In 1933—the year of his extension to the Rawlinson Building— he prepared a plan for completing the North Quadrangle which, had it been

[10] *Dictionary of National Biography 1971–81*, p. 560.
[11] SJCA, Mun. lxxxi. 176 (notes by Maufe on his work for the college).
[12] Colvin, *The Canterbury Quadrangle*, p. 106.
[13] SJCA, Mun. lxxxi. 82; see p. 123.

carried out, would have rendered some of the college's post-Second World War building projects unnecessary.[14] This scheme proposed the building of a new hall on the site of the President's stable block and a new quadrangle of residential buildings to the north, flanking St Giles and incorporating the seventeenth-century house now known as Middleton Hall, the lease of which was due to revert to the college in 1936.[15] But the new quadrangle was never built, and Middleton Hall, with its strange rear extension of red brick by Benjamin Woodward, architect of the Oxford University Museum, was turned instead into ten sets of undergraduate rooms.[16] The new hall was not built either, and in 1936 Maufe contrived extra seating in the existing Hall by creating a gallery over the Buttery and closing the former screens passage at the west end; a new route was then created from the Front to the North Quadrangle through the former ante-chapel, and is still in use.[17] As part of this project Maufe designed the wooden doors to the Chapel, with their vestigially Art Deco detailing, and he also rebuilt the Pinkerton Passage[18] that runs along the north side of the Hall and Chapel. But the North Quadrangle remained in its existing unsatisfactory state, with the presidential stable block protruding into its unfinished eastern side, and it was still in this state when the Second World War ended in 1945.

Before the Second World War St John's was an average-sized college with 180 junior and 16 senior members. Though it was less celebrated for academic prowess than its neighbour and rival, Balliol, its undergraduates nevertheless managed to gain eleven first-class degrees in 1939, a number equal to Balliol's and only exceeded by New College and Queen's.[19] Like most Oxford colleges, its revenues were derived overwhelmingly from land, both agricultural land, most of it in Oxfordshire and Berkshire, and urban property in Oxford, notably the North Oxford estate developed for middle-class housing after 1860. This garden suburb —in fact if not in name—brought in a steady stream of leasehold rents and offered the prospect of more substantial riches once the leases fell in; more recent developments on college land, including Belsyre Court in Woodstock Road (1934) and the Oxford Playhouse in Beaumont Street (Fig. 5), built to Maufe's designs in 1938, increased the rental income yet more. The Second World War wrenched British agriculture out of the depression into which it had sunk in the 1880s, and after the war the income from the college's farms—including a farm at Long Wittenham described in 1949 as a 'model of agricultural achievement'— continued to grow under the careful management of Ronald Hart-Synnot, Bursar

[14] SJCA, Mun. lxxxi. 80
[15] Before 1936 the house, which had been refronted in 1901–4, was leased to the Jesuits as Campion Hall: see G. Tyack, 'Baker and Lutyens in Oxford', Oxoniensia lxii (1997), pp. 297–308.
[16] St John's College Record (1936). The St Giles Façade of Middleton Hall is shown in Fig. 103, p. 119.
[17] See J. Mabbott, Oxford Memories (Oxford 1986), pp. 135–6.
[18] Named after J. S. Pinkerton (1813–91), Bursar in the mid-nineteenth century, when the original lean-to structure was built, see Fig. 11, p. 22.
[19] College Record (1939, 1952).

5 The Oxford Playhouse, by Edward Maufe, soon after completion in 1938. (© Oxfordshire County Council Photographic Archive)

since 1920.[20] Though not at the time one of the richest colleges in Oxford, St John's could face the post-war era with a fair degree of confidence.

That era was to be one of a steady growth in university education, which was to play a significant part in the social and economic transformation of Britain. Before the war a mere 51,000 students received a university education in the United Kingdom; by 1961 that number had doubled, to 113,000,[21] an expansion far in excess of the rate of growth of the British population as a whole. In Oxford the numbers increased over the same period from 4391 to 7396.[22] The growth in numbers began after the Butler Education Act of 1944 in response to a demand, first articulated by the wartime coalition government, for trained scientists, admin-istrators, technocrats, and teachers capable of managing the British economy and increasing its international competitiveness. Universities had always been training grounds for an administrative and professional elite. That ideal was now restated in the language of an age that believed in social and economic progress, fuelled by

[20] Hinchcliffe, *North Oxford*, pp. 187–8; *College Record* (1949).
[21] D. Chablo, 'University Architecture in Britain 1950–1975' (D. Phil. thesis, Oxford University, 1987), p. 1.
[22] P. Addison, 'Oxford and the Second World War' in B. Harrison (ed), *The History of Oxford University: the Twentieth Century* (1995), p. 187.

scientific research and technological innovation, and inspired by a belief in social improvement.

Numerical expansion coincided with a dramatic increase in government funding, most of it directed towards scientific research, some towards the payment of fees for poorer students, and some towards funding academic salaries. The University Grants Committee (UGC)—the agency that distributed government funding to universities—called in 1943 for university education to be made available to students from poorer social backgrounds, and in 1946 the Barlow Report on scientific manpower, commissioned during the Labour government of Clement Attlee, demanded a doubling in the number of students working for degrees in scientific and technological subjects. The expansion continued under the Conservatives, and in 1956 Anthony Eden's government proclaimed that 'all boys and girls who have the mental and general abilities to profit from a university education should get that opportunity'.[23] Maurice Bowra, Warden of Wadham College from 1938 to 1970, believed that government funding rescued Oxford University financially while at the same time improving its intellectual standards by increasing the numbers—and, perhaps the motivation—of candidates applying for undergraduate places.[24] So the Oxford of Evelyn Waugh's *Brideshead Revisited* became a willing client of the Welfare State.

More students, more academics teaching more subjects, more administrators: all this meant an ever-increasing demand for accommodation. Much of the demand came from the University, which, in the aftermath of the Second World War, was responsible for Oxford's laboratories and many of its libraries. Library provision in Oxford had already been greatly improved during the 1930s by the expansion of the Radcliffe Science Library (Hubert Worthington, 1933–4) and the building of the New Bodleian Library to the designs of Giles Gilbert Scott in 1937–40 (it was not opened until 1946). Now, following the end of the war, a sequence of UGC-funded buildings for scientific research and teaching went up in the 'Science Area' between South Parks Road and the University Parks: the departments of Botany and Forestry (Worthington 1947–50), and of Physiology (1949–53) and Inorganic Chemistry (1954–60), both by the firm of Lanchester and Lodge.[25] Stylistically conservative, like most British buildings in the immediate post-war years, these ponderous structures proclaimed the growing importance of the sciences in Oxford in a monumental if unadventurous manner.

Oxford had always relied on the colleges to house its students, and those who could not find housing in college were driven into the arms of the famous, or notorious, landladies. The return of ex-servicemen to complete their degrees after the war, together with the government-inspired drive to increase the number of university students, created something of a housing crisis, and by 1949–50 the

[23] Chablo, 'University Architecture', pp. 3–5.
[24] Harrison (ed), *History of Oxford University: the Twentieth Century*, p. 188.
[25] Tyack, *Oxford: an Architectural Guide*, pp. 290–2, 303.

proportion of students living out of college had risen from a pre-war figure of 40 per cent to more than half (52 per cent).[26] They included a growing number of postgraduate students, few of whom were given housing by their colleges, and it was partly with their needs in mind that the most important collegiate development of the immediate post-war years, Nuffield College, was begun in 1949 (it was completed in 1958).[27] Here, as in the new laboratories in South Parks Road, a self-consciously traditional style of architecture, related, at Lord Nuffield's insistence, to the Cotswold vernacular, disguised a building dedicated to novel purposes, in this case a postgraduate institution dedicated to research in the social sciences.

The growth of student numbers in Oxford could not fail to affect St John's. During the war the college shared its buildings with civil servants from the Ministry of Food, causing a later historian to call the North Quadrangle, where they were housed, 'the biggest fish and chip shop the world has ever seen';[28] by 1943, with the British armed services stretched to their full capacity, there were very few students in residence.[29] With the return to peacetime conditions numbers increased dramatically, with 131 housed in college and almost an equal number living outside in lodgings.[30] The election of four more fellows between 1939 and 1950—bringing the total to twenty—added to the overcrowding.[31] The pressure of numbers led to some changes in social habits. Before the war most undergraduates occupied two-roomed sets, with a separate bedroom and a sitting room to which their meals were sometimes brought by college servants (scouts). In order to squeeze more people into the college, some sets were now temporarily split into two separate bed-sitting rooms; the students meanwhile abandoned the practice of having meals in their rooms and resorted instead to the Hall.[32] But even with the maximum use of the existing accommodation, in Middleton Hall as well as in college, St John's remained crowded by pre-war standards. It clearly made sense to revive earlier plans for new building.

The college's first post-war building was not in the North Quadrangle, as might have been expected, but to the south of the Front Quadrangle. Here there was a yard on the long, narrow site of the Dolphin Inn, a stuccoed, timber-framed building which had been demolished in the late 1870s (Fig. 6), though its outbuildings survived to be used as student baths.[33] To the south was a narrow passageway leading into Trinity College, at the entrance to which Trinity commissioned plans from Hubert Worthington for a gatehouse block in his

[26] K. V. Thomas, 'College Life 1945–70', in Harrison, *op. cit.*, p. 192.
[27] The complicated history of the building is well told in Colvin, *Unbuilt Oxford*, pp. 166–177.
[28] Peter Hennessy, quoted in Harrison, *History of Oxford University: the Twentieth Century*, p. 170.
[29] *College Record* (1940, 1943).
[30] *College Record* (1946–7).
[31] Mabbott, *Oxford Memories*, p. 111.
[32] *College Record* (1951).
[33] See Withypool, *New Loggan*, p. 41. A photograph of the inn of c.1875 is illustrated in M. Graham and L. Waters, *Oxford Yesterday and Today* (Stroud, 1997), p. 56.

6 The former Dolphin Inn, with the entrance front of the college beyond. By the time the photograph was taken (c.1875) the buildings were used for undergraduate accommodation. They were demolished soon afterwards. (© Oxfordshire County Council Photographic Archive)

mannered Scandinavian-influenced style. Trinity's new building was to adjoin the southern end of the Dolphin site, and in April 1942 Ronald Hart-Synnot, the Bursar, wrote to Maufe suggesting that he and Worthington produce designs for a 'single piece of architecture . . . replacing the gruesome outhouses now existing by some appropriate building'.[34] If plans could be prepared now, it was hoped that work could start soon after the end of the war—an event the timing of which no one could predict with any certainty in 1942.

Maufe was an obvious choice as architect. Not only had he carried out a great deal of work for the college and made plans for the completion of the North Quadrangle; he had recently completed North Court at St John's College, Cambridge (1938–40), its reassuringly predictable brick elevations and pitched roofs calling to mind the loosely neo-Georgian blocks of flats designed by the London County Council's architect, G. Topham Forrest, during the inter-war years. Maufe told Hart-Synott that he would be glad to design a 'real building' for his own college and on 18 June 1942, having consulted Worthington,[35] he

[34] Mun. lxxxi. 45(1), 27 Apr. 1942.
[35] There was never any question of the building being jointly designed, or of holding a competition.

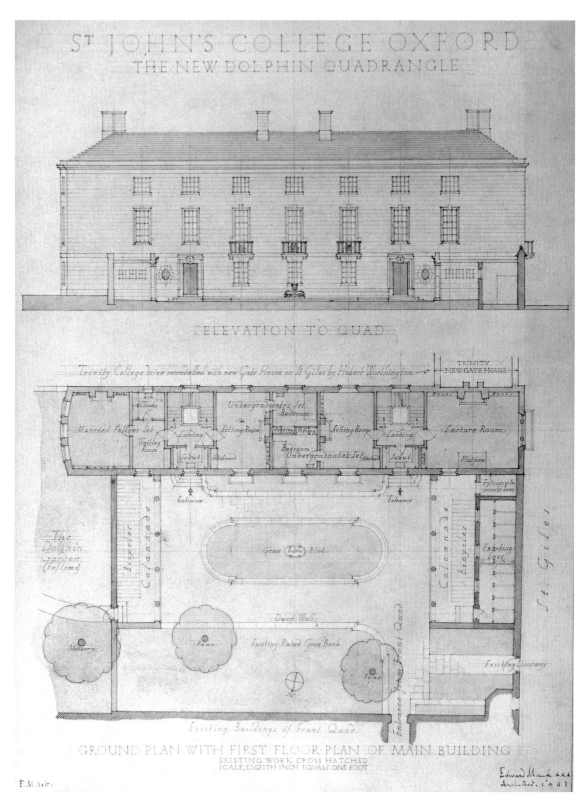

7 Edward Maufe's revised ground plan and elevation of the Dolphin Building, 1943

submitted plans for a three-storeyed neo-Georgian stone structure on the southern edge of the Dolphin site next to the Trinity boundary. The site was too narrow for a 'double pile' design, so the building would have to be one room deep, with a curved end to the east; it would contain baths and changing rooms, a lecture room, and seven sets of generously proportioned rooms for undergraduates and Fellows.[36] The height was intended to match that of the nearby Holmes Building, and the open space in front would be landscaped and enclosed on the east and west sides by colonnades, that on the west housing a bicycle shed and hiding an existing lavatory block. Hart-Synnot now told Maufe to incorporate three more sets by putting the bathrooms in a basement. 'We are building', he said, 'for several centuries, and the extra cost over that time will be negligible,' prompting Maufe to reply : 'I am naturally sorry that this building is not *exactly* what you want as I cannot help feeling that it is the best I have ever designed, but I have great hopes that I can satisfy the College and myself—the latter I always find the more difficult to deal with.' Later in the summer his revised design (Fig. 7) was approved by the college's Governing Body, made up of the tenured fellows under the chairmanship of the President, but the plans were shelved until the autumn of 1944, when £40,000 was set aside for the construction of what Hart-Synnot described as a 'good example of the best contemporary building'.[37]

The building of the Dolphin block was delayed until 1947 because of the severe restrictions imposed by the new Labour government elected in 1945. Its austerity programme was designed to divert physical and human resources towards what were deemed in Whitehall to be essential national purposes such as housing, the recovery of export markets, and the need to maintain the strength of the armed forces in a disturbingly uncertain post-war world. With stringent controls on manpower and materials in place, St John's had to persuade officials of the need for its new building at a time when more laboratory space was desperately needed in order to cater for the new emphasis on scientific research. Despite bureaucratic obstacles, Hart-Synnot was able to do this because he had already paid the local building firm of Benfield & Loxley to remove the 'overburden' from the limestone quarry at Clipsham (Rutland)—already used in the refacing of the Canterbury Quadrangle and selected by Maufe as most suitable for the new building—and had reserved 10,750 cubic feet of the underlying ashlar for the college's use.[38] There was also well-seasoned timber available from the college's own Bagley Wood, just south of Oxford, cut before war broke out.[39] Unlike the scientific departments, the college was not asking the government for money, and it could justifiably claim that it was assisting the government's aim of increasing the number of university students. The whole of Benfield & Loxley's workforce was employed in 1946 on Worthington's Forestry Laboratory in South Parks Road, but with its completion

---

[36] SJCA, Mun. lxxxi. 45(1), 7 May, 18 June (letters); lxxxi. 85(a) (plan and elevation).
[37] SJCA, Mun. lxxxi. 45(1), 24 June, 29 June, 1942, 3 Oct 1944; ADM I.A.11, p. 232.
[38] SJCA, Mun. lxxxi. 45(1), 15 Oct 1945.
[39] Mabbott, *Oxford Memories*, p. 110.

8 The Dolphin Quadrangle and the west entrance to the Dolphin Building (Chris Andrews)

in sight a contract was signed in February 1947 and work began in the following month. The building was ready for use in September 1948, at a total cost of £43,216, the excess over the original estimate of £40,000 being largely attributed to increases in the price of labour.[40]

Conceived during the Second World War and built in its straitened aftermath,

[40] SJCA, Mun. lxxxi. 45(1), 21 Dec 1945, 14 Feb, 27 Feb 1947; Mun. lxxxi. 45(2), 28 Oct 1949.

9 The façade of the Dolphin Building to St Giles, with the Trinity College gatehouse by Hubert Worthington next to it (Chris Andrews)

the Dolphin Building looks back, both aesthetically and in its generous planning, to the pre-war years.[41] Like his contemporaries Sir Albert Richardson and Raymond Erith, Maufe saw no need to adapt his architectural language to the dictates of the modernists who were already taking control of the schools of architecture. So, despite the use of concrete floors and an ingenious roof of terracotta pots to

[41] For a contemporary description of the building, see *Builder*, 14 Jan 1949, pp 47–54.

10 The sitting room of one of the sets in the Dolphin Building, 1949

circumvent the shortage of timber,[42] the building is unsurprisingly and un-demandingly conservative. The plain neo-Georgian north elevation (Fig. 8), facing the south or outer wall of the Front Quadrangle, echoes the façade of Maufe's nearby Oxford Playhouse, built ten years earlier in 1938, and, more distantly, the frontages of the adjoining 1820s houses in Beaumont Street. Maufe, though, did not possess the effortless understanding of classical proportions shown by the anonymous builders of the late Georgian era. His imagination was fired more by Gothic than classical architecture, and the detailing of the Dolphin Quadrangle has an awkwardness reminiscent in some ways of the work of Sir Herbert Baker, another architect who came to classicism from the Arts and Crafts tradition.[43] Doorways lead into the staircases at the east and west ends of the façade, their keystones embellished with carvings of dolphins, and at the centre of the first floor or *piano nobile* there are tall French windows leading onto metal balconies, their excessive height jarring with that of the more conventionally proportioned windows on either side. In the colonnades flanking the east and west sides of the courtyard Maufe had recourse to a stumpy and ill-proportioned version of the distinctive 'Bassae' Ionic order used with great panache and expertise by Charles Robert Cockerell in the Ashmolean and Taylorian building on the opposite side of St Giles, and visible from the courtyard. The Dolphin façade to St Giles is handled more successfully, with a balcony at first-floor level over a round-arched doorway leading into an electricity sub-station included at the insistence of the Oxford City

[42] Information from Sir Howard Colvin and Keith Pearce.
[43] As did Sir Edwin Lutyens, but his genius was of a different order.

Council (Fig. 9). But the main virtues of the building lie in the interiors, notably in the detailing of the limed oak staircases and of the ten sets of spacious and well-appointed rooms, including two studies for married Fellows (Fig. 10). Here memories of war and the experience of austerity were dissipated in the face of a reassuring continuity of gentlemanly values.

Maufe's architecture was admired in a post-war Oxford which valued continuity with the past and eschewed the challenge of architectural modernism. Hart-Synnot told him early in 1949: 'Praises continue to flow in about the Dolphin Quadrangle. Nearly every day some fresh expression of approval reaches me, and I would like you and your colleagues to know how much your skill is being appreciated.'[44] Maufe had by now become a leading member of the British architectural establishment. He was made principal architect to the Common-wealth War Graves Commission in 1943, he won the Royal Institute of British Architecture's Gold Medal in 1944, and he was knighted in 1954, following the completion of the Air Forces Memorial at Cooper's Hill overlooking Runnymede in Surrey (1950–3); together with the American Military Cemetery at Madingley, near Cambridge, this is the most impressive architectural memorial to the Second World War in Britain. Maufe's practice flourished after the war while those of many of his contemporaries languished, partly because of his official connections —with government, with the Inns of Court, with the older universities—but also because he offered a safe and reassuring style to an age which had felt that it had experienced enough change. This made it almost certain that he would fall foul of a younger and more iconoclastic generation, imbued with the excitement of architectural modernism, as he was soon to discover at his own *alma mater*, St John's.

[44] SJCA, Mun. lxxxi. 45(2), 3 Feb 1949.

2 A Hive of Learning: the Beehive Building

Modernist architecture did not make a significant impact on post-war Britain until the 1950s. The late 1940s were a time of austerity in which architecture was stifled by state-imposed controls and by the demands of the public sector, in which 40 per cent of architects worked.[1] But, three years after the election of a Conservative government in 1951, building licences were removed. Private and commercial building revived, and, in the already favoured public sector, funds at last became available for some of the more ambitious projects conceived in the aftermath of the war but deferred because of the lack of resources.

A new generation of architects moved forward to seize the opportunities now offered. During the 1930s a handful of British architects, emboldened by émigrés from abroad, had been converted to the doctrines of architectural modernism promulgated by the publicists of the 'International Style'. Convinced that a new age demanded a style of its own, they rejected existing styles, substituting for their rules and conventions a belief that both planning and external form should be determined by functional need. The new architecture should, they believed, aim for a radical simplicity, embracing and even expressing the technology that gave the modern age its progressive, experimental and innovative character. Their buildings—Owen Williams's Boots Factory at Nottingham, Lubetkin's Penguin Pool at the London Zoo and his Highpoint flats at Highgate, Mendelsohn and Chermayeff's De la Warr Pavilion at Bexhill-on-Sea, the Peter Jones store in Sloane Square, the houses of Maxwell Fry and Connell, Ward, and Lucas—were few in number and greatly outnumbered by the works of more conventional architects. But they captured the imagination of students at the architectural schools, some of which—notably the Architectural Association school in London—encouraged them to experiment in a similar fashion. As with many Continental avant-garde artistic groups, the success of the new style owed much to assiduous networking and publicity, by the Modern Architectural Research (MARS) group of architects and critics, founded in 1933, and through the pages of the *Architectural Review*.[2]

After the war the inter-war avant-garde overcame and superseded the architectural establishment. Schools of architecture that had until recently weaned their students on the classical Orders now expected them to embrace the design

---

[1] Chablo, 'University Architecture', p. 168.
[2] A. Jackson, *The Politics of Architecture* (London, 1970), pp. 28–35, 59; A. Saint, *Towards a Social Architecture* (New Haven and London 1987), pp. 2–5.

ideology of the Bauhaus, the rhetoric of Le Corbusier, and the gnomic utterances of Mies van der Rohe. Meanwhile an unprepared public accustomed to the drabness of Attlee's Britain found solace and visual excitement in the glass pavilions of the Festival of Britain in 1951.[3] As living standards improved during the 1950s, an architectural style that appeared to embody progress, to turn its back on a tainted past, and—so its apologists proclaimed—to proclaim the virtues of democracy and healthy living, began to command widespread acquiescence if not enthusiastic support. And as the costs of labour and materials steadily rose, the advantages of modern building technology and prefabrication became increasingly obvious. It was in this cultural climate that even the most conservative clients began to contemplate commissioning modernist designs.

Modernist architecture was slow in taking root in Oxford, though no slower than in many other places. Balliol and All Souls colleges commissioned designs for sleek International Style buildings during the 1930s,[4] but they were set aside. Cambridge was slightly more adventurous, and even succeeded in putting up one modernist building within the confines of an ancient college: Hughes and Bicknell's Fen Court at Peterhouse, completed (along with its own built-in air-raid shelter) in 1939. In the cautious climate of the post-war years new commissions in both of the ancient universities were entrusted to architects who could be relied upon to design buildings deemed to be in keeping with the spirit of the place. This meant the use of stone cladding and the employment of at least an approximation to the styles of the past, tempered in some instances by references to the inter-war architecture of the Low Countries and Scandinavia: the acceptable face of modernism for more traditionally minded clients. This state of affairs provoked the critic J. M. Richards, the leading theorist of modernist architecture in pre-war Britain, to write in 1952: 'There seems not to be, in either of the two old universities, any awareness of what is happening in the arts in the contemporary world, nor any marked sense of what are the contemporary issues.'[5]

In Oxford change was pioneered by the University, as part of its policy of filling the space south and west of the University Parks with government-funded science laboratories. Egged on by David Henderson, an economist at Lincoln College and Junior Proctor, the University's Committee for Buildings and Elevations was persuaded in 1955 to drop the safe and predictable firm of Lanchester and Lodge for the design of the new Dyson Perrins Laboratory for organic chemistry and to appoint in his place Basil Ward, one of the pioneering modernist architects who had established their reputations in the 1930s. His eight-storeyed tower block and lecture room was begun in 1957, and in the next few years he superseded

[3] Jackson, *The Politics of Architecture*, pp. 176–8. See also E. Harwood and A. Powers (eds), *Festival of Britain* (London, 2001).
[4] H. M. Colvin, *Unbuilt Oxford*, pp. 160–6. The architects were Maxwell Fry (All Souls) and Samuel and Harding (Balliol).
[5] 'Recent Building in Oxford and Cambridge', *Architectural Review* (Aug. 1952), p. 73. Richards was the author of the influential *An Introduction to Modern Architecture*, first published by Pelican Books in 1940.

Lanchester and Lodge as the dominating architectural presence both in the Science Area and in the 'Keble Road Triangle' to the west, sold by St John's to the University and given over to the needs of Oxford's engineers.[6]

Modernist architecture made its first tentative appearance at St John's with the enlargement of the Senior Common Room in 1953–5. Here Maufe was asked to prepare designs in 1951, but he withdrew rather than accepting amendments proposed by the Bursar, Arthur Garrard, the former Surveyor-General of the Duchy of Lancaster's estates, who had replaced Hart-Synnot in 1949. The commission was then handed over, with Maufe's agreement, to David Booth of the locally based firm of Booth and Ledeboer.[7] And it was Booth who designed the facade of the Common Room to the President's garden: a graceless exercise in architectural minimalism which itself has now (2004) fallen victim to a new and more glamorous design from the office of MacCormac, Jamieson and Prichard.[8] Booth was not asked in 1956 to design the long-awaited set of undergraduate rooms that would complete the North Quadrangle, and a proposal to reinstate Maufe for this important commission provoked a reaction which was to lead to the creation of one of the most strikingly original English university buildings of its time.

The decision to resume building in the North Quadrangle (Fig. 11) came in response to the continuing government-inspired drive for more university graduates. Though operating a deficit, the college had nevertheless undertaken in 1952 to increase the number of junior members by 10 per cent to about 230.[9] By this time the overcrowding that had been a feature of the immediate post-war years had disappeared and St John's had resumed something of its inter-war tranquillity. But with rentable property in the City of Oxford at a premium—the result of post-war restraints on expansion and of political pressure to use local housing for local residents—it was clear that housing for between twenty and thirty more students would soon be needed, together with space for some at least of the growing number of Fellows, of whom there were twenty-two by 1953. A Development Committee was therefore set up in 1956 by the Governing Body, made up of the President—Austin Lane Poole—the Bursar, and four Fellows: the constitutional historian W. C. Costin, who became President when Poole retired in 1957; J. D. Mabbott, a philosopher who succeeded Costin as President in 1963; Harold Thompson (a chemist and Fellow of the Royal Society), and George Richardson, an economist who later was to become Warden of Keble College.[10] It recommended that a new block housing between twenty-five and thirty people should be built on the site of the old presidential stables (Fig. 12) at a suggested

[6]   Colvin, *Unbuilt Oxford*, p. 179.
[7]   SJCA, ADM I.A. 11, pp. 332, 342; Mun. lxxxi. 50; *College Record* (1953).
[8]   See p. 000.
[9]   *College Record* (1952). The deficit was meanwhile mitigated by an increase in tuition fees: Hinchcliffe, *North Oxford*, p. 195.
[10] Sillery, *St John's College Biographical Register 1919–75*, passim.

11 The North Quadrangle looking south in c.1955. The Senior Common Room is on the left and the Hall and Chapel to the right, entered through the Pinkerton Passage in front, remodelled by Maufe in 1936. (Architects' Co-Partnership)

cost of £80,000—a generous budget by the standards of the time. The bulk of the funding would be furnished by the sale of government stocks and land in Marston Ferry Road in North Oxford, the remainder coming from sales of the house property that still made up 70 per cent of the college's external income; the fees from the extra students would compensate for the loss of leasehold rental income.[11]

Sir Edward Maufe, as he had become in 1954, had first drawn up plans for replacing the stables with new buildings in the 1930s.[12] After the completion of his Dolphin Quadrangle in 1948 he had overseen the completion of the stone refacing scheme in the Canterbury Quadrangle, begun in the 1930s,[13] and he also designed the surface layout of the Front Quadrangle with its central lawn surrounded by cobbles and flagstones, completed in time for the 400th anniversary of the college's foundation in 1955.[14] As the college's architectural elder statesman, and an Honorary Fellow, it would have been surprising if he had not been consulted about the projected building in the North Quadrangle. He had already been asked to make plans for the layout and resurfacing of this Quadrangle,[15] and in May 1956 he was duly invited by the Bursar to submit designs.[16]

---

[11] SJCA, Mun. lxxxi. 59, 9 Nov 1956; Hinchcliffe, *North Oxford*, p. 196.
[12] See above, pp. 6–7.
[13] W. A. Oakeshott (ed), *Oxford Stone Restored* (Oxford, 1975), p. 102.
[14] *College Record* (1955).
[15] SJCA, ADM I.A. 11, p. 44; Mun. lxxxii. 226.   [16] SJCA, Mun. lxxxi. 153.

12 The President's stables in the North Quadrangle shown shortly before their replacement by the Beehive Building

But six months later, on 14 November, the Governing Body agreed to refer the choice of architect back to the Development Committee, whose membership was significantly changed by the replacement of Costin – who had been elected to his fellowship soon after the First World War—with one of the younger fellows, Howard Colvin.[17] Colvin brought with him architectural interests and expertise rarely present in Oxford's senior common rooms. He began his academic life as a historian of the Middle Ages, but in 1954 he published the first edition of his *Biographical Dictionary of English Architects 1660–1840*, on which his subsequent reputation as one of England's leading architectural historians has rested.[18] No admirer of Maufe's architecture, he believed that the new project demanded 'a frankly contemporary treatment which would make no concessions to the adjoining buildings except in such matters as scale and material'.[19] Equally important, Maufe's proposal to continue his 'all but lifeless' 1933 building southwards would in Colvin's view have created a disagreeably 'broken-backed' effect at the junction with the north wall of the Senior Common Room, which is not in alignment with the south wall of Maufe's staircase 19.[20] Backed by some of his colleagues on the Committee, Colvin now asked his fellow architectural historian Sir John Summerson—a member of the MARS group in the 1930s and latterly

[17] SJCA, ADM I.A. 11, p. 420. Colvin came to St John's in 1948.
[18] It was subsequently enlarged as the *Biographical Dictionary of British Architects 1600–1840* and went through two more editions. For the genesis of the project, see Colvin, *Essays in English Architectural History* (New Haven and London, 1999), pp. 292–4.
[19] SJCA, Mun. lxxxi. 59, 24 Nov 1956.
[20] Colvin, *Unbuilt Oxford*, pp. 180–1.

curator of Sir John Soane's Museum—for suggestions of names of alternative architects. Summerson responded with the names of four firms, none of whom were, in his reassuring words, 'New Brutalists or in any way shocking':[21] a reference to a term applied by the critic and historian Reyner Banham to the group of young architects associated with Alison and Peter Smithson, *enfants terribles* of British avant-garde architectural discourse in the mid-1950s. The architects sent Colvin photographs of their work, and on 5 December the Governing Body voted by 11 to 4 to commission a new design. Two days later Garrard broke the news to Maufe: 'I hope you will realise how difficult it is for me to write this letter and how much I regret having to do it. The younger Fellows are determined, however, and feel . . . that it is the duty of the College to provide the opportunity for doing important work to someone who, while not unknown, has not made his name'.[22]

The decision to drop Maufe marked a decisive break with the tradition of gentlemanly architectural patronage at St John's. It also opened the way to choosing a design which was revolutionary, in an Oxford where modernist architecture was still unknown. Only one of the architects now under consideration was a traditionalist. Raymond Erith was described by Summerson as 'a reincarnation of Soane', and 'the only living person who can really do classical mouldings'; he was later to design Oxford's finest post-war classical buildings—the Provost's Lodgings of The Queen's College (1958–9) and the Library at Lady Margaret Hall (1959–61).[23] The other three firms all worked in the modernist style. H. T. Cadbury-Brown was, said Summerson, 'a delightful man with a quiet, subtle talent', best known for the design of schools: a staple of many architectural practices in the early days of the Welfare State. Chamberlin, Powell and Bon had also designed a primary school (Bousfield Primary School, 1954–6) in Bolton Gardens, Kensington, which attracted much favourable notice and which Summerson thought was 'quite brilliant'. But they were best-known for their housing schemes, notably the Golden Lane estate and the adjacent Barbican estate in the City of London, for which they were selected as architects in 1955 (work began in 1963). Peter Chamberlin, one of the partners, told Colvin that 'St John's deserves a live architectural solution to its building problems, rather than some stylistic reproduction which, although intended to flatter the old, usually fails badly'.[24] The firm later had an opportunity to put these ideas into practice at New Hall, Cambridge (1962–6), and in several other university commissions, notably the University of Leeds, where their Roger Stevens Building is one of the most extraordinary examples of architectural expressionism of the 1960s. But at St John's it faced stiff competition from the fourth of Summerson's recommendations, the Architects' Co-Partnership. Summerson told Colvin that 'the ACP men are educated (e.g. they buy, read & discuss our books!)', and this may have played a part in the Development

[21] Letter to Howard Colvin, 12 Nov. 1956.
[22] SJCA, Mun. lxxxi. 59, Garrard to Maufe 7 Dec 1956.
[23] See L. Archer, *Raymond Erith, Architect* (Burford 1985).
[24] SJCA, Mun. lxxxi. 153, Chamberlin to Colvin, 28 Nov 1956.

13 Michael Powers
(Alan Powers)

Committee's decision at a meeting, attended by Summerson, on 21 December 1956, to ask Michael Powers (Fig. 13), one of the founding partners of the firm, to prepare sketch designs and elevations for the new building. In writing to Powers, the Bursar expressed some misgivings about the firm's architecture:

> We were all greatly impressed by the imaginative elevations: but the Committee was frankly a little apprehensive about asking you to prepare plans on the evidence which these pictures provided, and I think you appreciated the difficulty of visualizing an elevation which would harmonize with buildings in the North Quad when confronted only with pictures of factories, etc.[25]

But the sketch designs, submitted in January 1957, met with the Committee's approval, and Powers was asked to prepare a set of detailed designs.

Founded in 1939, the Architects' Co-Partnership started off as a team of eleven architects trained at the Architectural Association school in London—the main nursery of modernist architecture in England—during the 1930s.[26] During their student years they had learned to value the study of sociology, technology, and planning over the minute understanding of the works of classical antiquity esteemed by an older generation of teachers. Le Corbusier himself had written in the AA student journal in 1938: 'Architecture is organisation. You are an organiser,

---

[25] SJCA, Mun. lxxxi. 153, Garrard to Powers, 21 Dec 1956, 12 Jan 1957.
[26] By 1956 the firm was made up of seven of the original partners—C. K. Capon, P. L. Cocke, M. H. Cooke-Yarborough, A. W. Cox, L. M. de Syllas, J. M. Grice and Michael Powers, together with three associates.

14 The interior of the Brynmawr Rubber Factory (The Twentieth Century Society)

not a drawing-board stylist.'[27] Taking their cue from the Bauhaus architects and from the Tecton firm founded by Berthold Lubetkin—perhaps the most talented member of the English modernist avant-garde in the 1930s—the partners intended to supplant the ideal of the individual 'art-architect', represented by such figures as Maufe, by that of the architect as a member of a team devoted to the good of society. Even the term 'co-partnership' reflects the high-minded serious-ness of the early twentieth-century Garden City pioneers. As Anthony Cox, one of the partners, later wrote:

> It is not surprising that the notion of working together as a group came naturally to the founders of ACP. It was not only because they rejected the concept of the architect as prima donna dominating the supporting cast, but more fundamentally because they thought a combination of like-minded architects on an equal footing could examine problems more deeply, cover a greater range of expertise and produce more rational and efficient solutions.[28]

Such idealism was encouraged by the collectivism of the Second World War and the subsequent drive for social and physical reconstruction under Attlee's government. It was in this climate of opinion that the firm made its name in

[27] Quoted in V. Perry, *Built for a Better Future: the Brynmawr Rubber Factory* (Oxford 1994), p. 32.
[28] [A. Cox], *Architects Co-partnership: the First 50 Years* (privately published, 1989).

1948–52 through the design of the Brynmawr Rubber Factory (since demolished) on an industrial estate in a depressed mining valley in South Wales (Fig. 14). With its spectacular interior, roofed by nine shell-concrete domes, it soon became an icon of the Modern movement in Britain, and was seen by many observers as a model of that marriage of technical skill, human ingenuity, and social idealism that would, it was hoped, transform society as a whole.

The firm subsequently built up a reputation as designers of schools, not only in Britain—including several in Hertfordshire, where the local authority encouraged prefabricated modernist designs—but also the West Indies, the Middle East and Africa (there was an office in Lagos). As one one of the partners later wrote:

ACP was not so much concerned with creating architectural monuments as with the provision of humane and efficient shelter for social activities and by accident rather than design found itself building for education, following the post-war bulge in the birth rate, through primary to secondary schools, generally using pre-fabricated methods of construction.[29]

The commission for the new building at St John's came soon after the ACP had made its first foray into university architecture with the design of a complex of chemistry buildings at the University of Leicester, which went up between 1958 and 1961.[30] The firm had already secured a foothold in Oxford with their rebuilding of the President's Lodgings at Corpus Christi College (completed in 1958), the somewhat unprepossessing entrance front of which was enthusiastically described by the architectural historian Mark Girouard as the first post-war building 'to proclaim to the outside world that Oxford has stopped playing for safety'.[31] But St John's was to be its first residential building for undergraduates, and it gave Michael Powers the opportunity to rethink the layout and form of an Oxford collegiate residence in a radical manner which reflected the egalitarian spirit of the times.

The Governing Body resolved on 16 January 1957 that it was no longer necessary to make the rooms large enough to dine and entertain guests, though the question of whether they should be bed-sitting rooms or two-roomed sets—preferred by most of the Fellows—was left open to negotiation, as was the question of staircase or corridor access.[32] Powers opted for 31 bed-sitting rooms, along with three sets of rooms for Fellows. His first thoughts were too revolutionary for some of the older members the college, as J. D. Mabbott, one of the senior members of the Development Committee, recalled in his memoirs:

[29] A. L. Morgan and C. Naylor (eds), *Contemporary Architects* (Chicago and London 1987), pp. 41–3, where the schools are listed. For the firm's contribution to the school-building programme, see A. Saint, *Towards a Social Architecture*, pp. 76–7, 164. By 1959 the firm had designed 34 schools.
[30] N. Pevsner and E. Williamson, *The Buildings of England: Leicestershire* (London, 1992), p. 259.
[31] M. Girouard, 'An Oxford President's House Replanned', *Country Life*, (8 Dec 1960), pp. 1440–1.
[32] SJCA, ADM I.A.11, pp. 425–6.

In due course the plans and models came along. They showed a building exactly like a new suburban secondary school or a modern hygienic factory—a rectangle box, with a flat roof, unbroken horizontal lines, lots of glass. The old conservatives of the pro-Maufe party said 'What a horror! We told you so! But now you've had it. No going back now.' So we got the architect, Michael Power [*sic*], to come along and take us through the details. Yes, he had given us all we asked for—thirty rooms, three Fellows' sets, lavish bathrooms, etc. We asked about access to the rooms. 'Well,' said Michael Power 'up the staircase at the end there and then corridors.' There was a gasp of horror and revulsion. 'What? Can't have that! Can't have that! Can't have corridors in St. John's!' . . . 'Women's Colleges have corridors! Keble has corridors!' What did we want then? Staircases! Staircases![33]

Powers presented the college with two alternative corridor-less designs during the spring of 1957. One was for an L-shaped building with a 'double pile' arrangement of rooms in a main block running north and south, and a narrower wing projecting forward into the quadrangle from the north end (Fig. 15).[34] The other, for which a preliminary drawing survives, shows a single block with zigzag edges and hexagonal rooms (Fig. 16), anticipating the 'Beehive' block that was eventually built. This highly original design seems to have been first conceived by an unknown member of the ACP team,[35] a natural turn of events in a group practice where designs were entrusted to an individual partner but subjected to group discussion and criticism.[36] Writing thirty years later, however, Mabbott gave the main credit to Powers himself:

Michael Power was a lively young man and he said 'Oh I see! Well, thirty rooms. That means three staircases, ten rooms on each.' We agreed and he said at once that he could not do it in the space available. He had only just found room for one staircase with difficulty. We told him we were in no hurry and asked him to go away and think about it. He came back with his second thought—the fascinating block of hexagon rooms giving (as the bees know) the greatest possible economy of space, and three staircases.[37]

Both designs were shown to Maufe, who wrote in predictably unenthusiastic terms to Garrard: 'I am sorry I am not more happy about these schemes. I was prepared for modern fenestration and would have welcomed it, but I was not prepared for the plans to be so unfunctional in so many different ways.'[38] Powers told the Governing Body that the 'Beehive' scheme was more expensive than the L-shaped one, but that it was intrinsically strong and self-bracing and could be of light contruction, making it 'more economical than reproducing in style any of the types of building already in the Quad'.[39] But despite its greater cost it was the 'Beehive' design that was selected, not only because of its intrinsic ingenuity but also because

[33] *Oxford Memories* (Oxford, 1986), pp. 137–8.
[34] There are uncatalogued drawings in the Muniment Room, dated 14 March and 16 April 1957.
[35] Information from Sir Howard Colvin.
[36] Chablo, 'University Architecture', p. 205; [A. Cox], *Architects' Co-partnership: the First 50 Years.*
[37] *Oxford Memories*, p. 138.
[38] SJCA, Mun. lxxxi. 59, 2 May 1957.
[39] SJCA, Mun. lxxxi. 153, 6 May 1957.

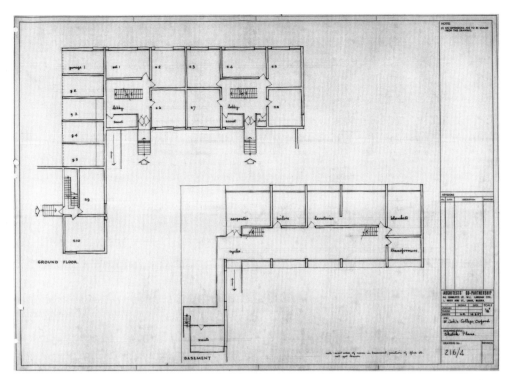

15 A design for the east side of the North Quadrangle by the Architects' Co-Partnership, basement and ground-floor plans, March 1957 (Architects' Co-Partnership)

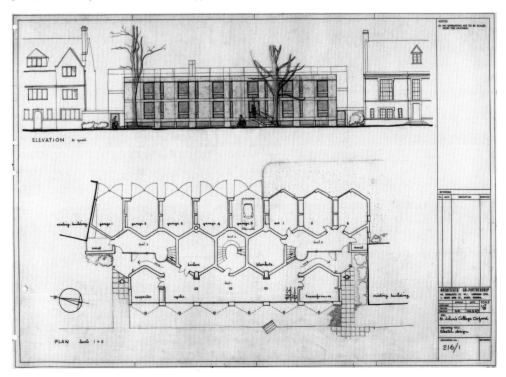

16 An early version of the Beehive design, March 1957 (Architects' Co-Partnership)

of its greater adaptability to the site, the irregularities of which are masked by the two ranges of hexagonal rooms (Fig. 17).[40] Powers now produced a revised version of this design, which took into account some of Maufe's objections,[41] and at the end of May Maufe told Garrard: 'I am glad that some of my criticisms have been dealt with and now hope for the best. I will put in some prayers for Mr Powers.'[42] More modifications took place over the next few months,[43] especially on the ground floor of the garden side, where what was originally intended as a garage for the President's car (Fig. 18) was given over to Fellows' rooms. Work began in the summer of 1958, when a contract was signed with the firm of Benfield and Loxley, builders of the Dolphin Quadrangle. The building was completed early in 1960.[44]

The concept of a building as a beehive has long fascinated both architects and patrons. Richard Foxe, Bishop of Winchester, expressed the hope that his new foundation of Corpus Christi College, Oxford (1517), would be a hive where 'the scholars night and day may make wax and sweet honey in honour of God, and the advantage of themselves and all Christian men'.[45] Ever since the Middle Ages the metaphor of a beehive has appealed to philosophers inclined to view human society as a communal organism rather than an agglomeration of competing individuals. And for some architects of a utopian turn of mind the beehive has been seen as a paradigm of an organic community. Beehive analogies have recently been discerned in some of the work of the Catalan architect Antonio Gaudí, notably in his only partially completed chapel of the Colonia Güell in Barcelona, and also in

---

[40] Information from Sir Howard Colvin.
[41] Uncatalogued drawings in the Muniment Room, dated 28 May 1957.
[42] SJCA, Mun. lxxxi. 59, 27 May 1957, 31 May 1957.
[43] Uncatalogued drawings in the college muniments dated Dec 1957.
[44] SJCA, Mun. lxxxi. 153, 21 May 1958.
[45] For the Latin original, see T. Fowler, *The History of Corpus Christi College* (Oxford: Oxford Historical Society, 1899), p. 38.

Sketch I without windows.

December 1957
Architects' Co-partnership
MP

18 A sketch design by Michael Powers for the garden front of the Beehive, December 1957. The garage space on the ground floor was later given over to rooms. Booth and Lederboer's Senior Common Room extension (completed in 1955) is to the left

Bruno Taut's famous Glass Pavilion for the Deutsche Werkbund exhibition at Cologne in 1914.[46] In the modernist architecture that was espoused by Powers and his contemporaries design was driven not by pre-existing stylistic conventions but by a programme or concept.[47] For Powers that underlying concept was the honeycomb.

A possible influence on the choice of the beehive, or honeycomb, design for St John's is the work of Frank Lloyd Wright. During the 1930s Wright developed an interest in 'organic' architecture, a notoriously imprecise concept which he expounded in a series of lectures given in London in 1939, the year the Architects' Co-Partnership was founded.[48] For Wright organic architecture was 'natural architecture—the architecture of nature, for nature'. His search for 'natural' forms and means of expression led him to make increasing use of materials such as wood and stone, as in his Taliesin West in Arizona, and also to experiment with the hexagonal or honeycomb plan. The hexagon was, he believed, 'a direct plan for simple living' which could play a part in the development of what he called an 'architecture of social reflex' conducive to human happiness. All corners of a hexagon, he wrote in 1938,

are obtuse as in a honeycomb. Therefore a pattern more natural to human movement is

[46] J. A. Ramirez, *The Beehive Metaphor* (London, 2000), pp. 60–6, 102–5.
[47] See J. Summerson 'The Case for a Theory of "Modern" Architecture', reprinted in *The Unromatic Castle* (London, 1990), pp. 263–4.
[48] They are printed in F. L. Wright, *The Future of Architecture* (New York, 1963), pp. 239–341. See especially pp. 244–7.

the result. Interiors have more reflex. Therefore more repose... [The] cross-section of a honeycomb has more fertility and flexibility where human movement is concerned than the square. The obtuse angle is more suited to human 'to and fro' than the right angle.[49]

These ideas reached their fruition in a house he built in 1936–7 for the educationist Paul Hanna and his wife on the Stanford University campus at Palo Alto, California.[50] This low, spreading building is based on a hexagonal grid expressed internally in the floor tiles. The rooms, with their serrated walls of timber and glass, are grouped around a central brick core containing the kitchen, and overlook a typically Californian *rus in urbe* of hills and dense Mediterranean-style vegetation (Figs. 19–20). Thereafter hexagonal grids, with their implicit challenge to the insistent rectilinearity of much European modernist architecture, became a feature of Wright's highly original and idiosyncratic late style.

The beehive design at St John's is related to some of Wright's later work, even if it was not directly influenced by it; the American-born Powers owned a copy of *Organic Architecture* (1939),[51] and the publication of Bruno Zevi's *Towards an Organic Architecture* (1950) introduced Wright's later buildings to a wide audience of architects and critics.[52] But there are also European analogies. The German architect Hugo Häring had stated in 1925 that '[if] we want to find forms which are not artificial, we shall discover them in accordance with nature,' and both he and his compatriot Hans Scharoun designed buildings with non-rectangular, if not strictly hexagonal, rooms, their windows slanted to catch the sunlight.[53] There is also a parallel to the studied picturesqueness of some post-war Scandinavian buildings, much admired by the English 'New Empiricist' architects of the early 1950s.[54] The *Architectural Review* pointed out a connection between the serrated wall surfaces of the Beehive and those of the recently built training college for the Association of Swedish Employers, designed in a woodland setting near Stockholm by the Swedish architect Anders Tengbom and drawing its inspiration, as the writer fancifully put it, from 'the ultimate source of the collegiate ideal: the Grove of Academe'.[55] A closer parallel to the Beehive is provided by David Roberts's exactly contemporary Castle Hill Hostel for Clare College, Cambridge (1957–8) (Fig. 21),[56] though neither it nor the Swedish building has hexagonal rooms. And Basil Spence's Coventry Cathedral (finished in 1962), perhaps the most popular and certainly the most publicized English building of its period, has serrated walls

[49] *Architectural Record* (July 1938), quoted in R. Joncas, 'Pedagogy and "Reflex": Frank Lloyd Wright's Hanna House Revisited', *Journal of the Society of Architectural Historians* liii(3), (Sept. 1993), p. 313.
[50] The genesis of the house is discussed in Joncas, 'Pedagogy and "Reflex"', pp. 307–22. See also Ramirez, *Beehive Metaphor*, pp. 109–15.
[51] Information from Alan Powers.
[52] William Whyte tells me that Louis Kahn was also interested in hexagonal planning.
[53] J. Joedicke, *Architecture since 1945* (London 1969), pp. 52–61.
[54] As Nicholas Bullock points out (*Building the Post-war World*, London 2000, p. 47), there is a connection between Wright's 'organic architecture' and the New Empiricism.
[55] *Architectural Review* 127 (June 1960), pp. 376–80.
[56] *Architectural Review* 125 (June 1959), pp. 382–5; N. Taylor and P. Booth, *Cambridge New Architecture* (1970), pp. 114–15.

19 The exterior of the Hanna House, Stanford, California, by Frank Lloyd Wright (Geoffrey Tyack)

20 The interior of the Hanna House, Stanford, California, by Frank Lloyd Wright, showing the hexagonal floor tiles (Geoffrey Tyack)

designed to direct light towards the high altar. In this sense the Beehive, for all its unconventional planning, is very much a building of its time.

Contemporary architectural critics were impressed by the way in which the Beehive introduced modernist architecture into a historic setting. The *Architects' Journal* saw the building was an example of *architecture parlante*, expressing 'the

21 Castle Hill Hostel for Clare College, Cambridge, by David Roberts (Cambridge 2000)

cellular character of a Hall of Residence',[57] the cell here presumably meaning a monastic rather than a biological cell (Fig. 22) . The plan was also said to have arisen 'from a desire to provide a broken skyline for the building, which would continue the Oxford tradition of spires, gables and pinnacles without recourse to the application of ornament'.[58] The Beehive certainly has a picturesque quality that sets it apart from the angularity and hardness admired by the New Brutalists and celebrated in the Smithsons' much photographed school at Hunstanton (Norfolk), completed in 1954. It could even be said to fit into the 'townscape' tradition expounded with the help of seductive drawings by Gordon Cullen in the pages of the *Architectural Review* during the 1950s.[59] The exponents of 'townscape' argued for a revival of the values of the eighteenth-century Picturesque: variety, surprise, irregularity, varied surfaces. These qualities are all found in the North Quadrangle, and they help give the Beehive its distinctive character.[60]

The design was carefully modulated so that there are two storeys over a sunken semi-basement (used as bicycle shed) facing the North Quadrangle, and three to the President's garden; the object was to reduce the height of the building on the quadrangle side (Fig. 23). The rooms are ranged on either side of a central core containing top-lit brick-clad staircases (Fig. 24) and lavatories. The internal structure is of concrete, with partition walls of brick, and the concrete floors contained under-floor heating panels: another idea found in Wright's work, though

[57] 17 Nov 1960, p. 727.
[58] *Architectural Review* 128 (Aug. 1960), p. 106; *Architects' Journal* (17 Nov 1960), p. 730.
[59] Cullen did an unexecuted design, with the encouragement of Howard Colvin, for the layout of the Front Quadrangle, as an alternative to Maufe's layout: SJCA, Mun. lxxxi. 86.
[60] *Architectural Review* 128 (Sept 1960), p. 104.

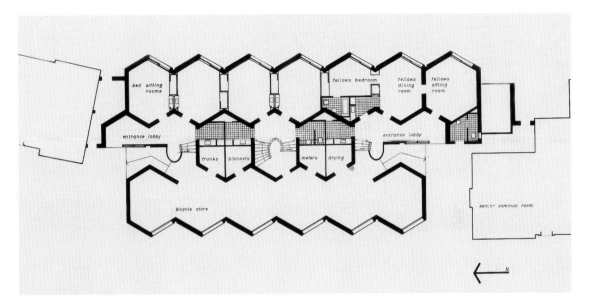

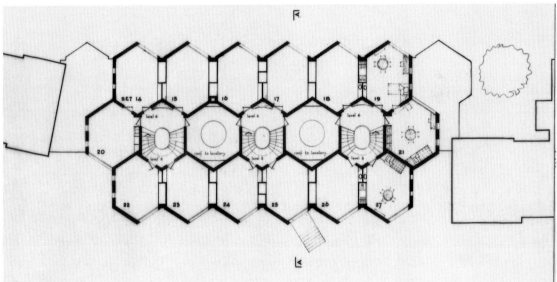

22 Ground and first-floor plans of the Beehive Building (Architects' Co-Partnership)

uncommon in England in the 1950s.[61] Each room has two external faces, one made up of sliding double-glazed windows in aluminium frames with blackened panels of stippled glass underneath, the other of stone over a granite plinth.[62] The serrated external walls express the internal shape of the rooms, and the windows are placed so as to catch the sunlight: from the south-east on the garden side (Fig. 25) and the south-west on the side facing the quadrangle, where the occupants enjoy a view of the activity outside, thus encouraging the communal values which

[61] They were subsequently removed and a more conventional heating system introduced: information from Tom Sherwood.
[62] *Architectural Review* 128 (Aug 1960), pp. 106–7.

23 A cross-section of the Beehive and North Quadrangle, May 1957 (Architects' Co-Partnership)

24 One of the staircases in the Beehive (Chris Andrews)

25 The Beehive from the President's garden, looking north soon after completion. Maufe's staircase 19 is on the right (Architects' Co-Partnership)

26 The North Quadrangle with the Beehive, and the Rawlinson Building (1909–11) to the left (Architects' Co-Partnership)

both the college and the architects wished to foster (Fig. 26). The roofs are not flat, like those of so many contemporary modernist buildings, but pointed, and the turrets over the central staircases, with their clerestory-like windows, evoke the lantern towers of some medieval churches. But, with the exception of the spikes on top of the staircase turrets, decoration, as conventionally understood, is non-existent. Frank Lloyd Wright had believed that the form of a building should be determined by 'the simple laws of common sense' and 'the nature of materials, the nature of purpose [being] so well understood that a bank will not look like a Greek temple, a university will not look like a cathedral, nor a fire-engine house

27 The North Quadrangle, showing the Rawlinson Building (N. W. Harrison), staircase 19 (Maufe) and the north end of the Beehive (Chris Andrews)

resemble a French chateau, or what have you. Form follows function? Yes, but more important now, *form and function are one.*[63] This merging of form and function occurred in the Beehive, as it did later in the Sir Thomas White Building.

The decision to use stone rather than brick or concrete for the outer walls was made by the college,[64] but the stone was chosen by the architect. His choice was, in an Oxford context, a surprising one: Portland, with Cornish slate for the roofs.[65] In refacing its older buildings—a major project during the 1950s and 1960s—St John's used the yellowish limestone from Clipsham, and the same stone was employed by Maufe in his Dolphin building. Clipsham stone would have matched the Ancaster limestone of the Rawlinson Building on the north side of the North Quadrangle, and the Taynton of Scott's Building on the western side. Portland stone, by contrast, was white not yellow, and it ensured that the building would stand out from, rather than blend in with, its surroundings (Fig. 27): something which those who value gentlemanly restraint and 'good taste' over architectural creativity have always found hard to forgive. Portland stone was not unknown in Oxford—it had, for instance, been used for the columns and dressings of the Ashmolean Museum, begun in 1841. But, despite its attractive surface texture and its durability, it had

[63] *The Future of Architecture*, p. 246.
[64] SJCA, ADM. I.A.11, pp. 425–6; *Guardian*, 10 Oct. 1960.
[65] *Architectural Review* (Sept 1969). Howard Colvin was 'never quite happy' with the choice.

rarely been chosen in the past, partly because of the availability of other kinds of stone closer to hand, partly because it was thought that it would stand out disagreeably against the differently-coloured local stones usually employed.[66] For the Beehive a shell-rich vein from the Roach beds was selected, enhancing the textural character of the building. The Roach beds are found above the more commonly used Whitbed beds, the stone from which can be seen all over London. Roach stone was more difficult to cut than Whitbed, making it 25 per cent more expensive, but it was very durable.[67] And by choosing Portland stone at St John's the Architects' Co-Partnership started a fashion which lasted through the 1960s, notably in the work of the firm of Powell and Moya, who were responsible for some of the most distinguished Oxford buildings of the period.[68] Powers's drawings show the care with which the stone was placed, and the texture of the building can still give pleasure to the sympathetic observer.

The Beehive was not a cheap building. The total cost was £81,700 (only just over budget) or a generous £2,023 per room; more than twice the figure of £726–£924 laid down by the University Grants Committee in the 1960s, though the cost per room was much less than that of the Dolphin Building. The rooms were 200 feet square, half as large again as the University Grants Committee had recommended for government-funded student residences in 1948 and nearly twice the average size in the mid-1960s.[69] The *Oxford Mail* thought that they were 'astonishingly spacious' and quoted a college servant who said: 'I would far rather work on this staircase than any of the old ones. They are easy to keep tidy, and when you've cleaned them you can see they are clean.'[70] The rooms were panelled throughout in wood, after the Scandinavian fashion popular during the 1950s, and the ceilings were of pine matchboard (Fig. 28). The furnishing—comfortable chairs of Scandinavian design and English hand-made items—was jointly decided by the college and Powers. Though criticized by the *Architects' Journal* for being too 'genteel and refined'[71] by the *Observer* for exuding 'bourgeois politeness',[72] and by some of the occupants for inadequate sound insulation—the walls separating the rooms are broken only by cupboards and wash-basins (Fig. 29)—the Beehive rooms nevertheless represented a degree of comfort which many of the early occupants, many of whom were young grammar-school-educated men from humdrum lower-middle-class backgrounds—had not experienced before. These fortunate youths were the beneficiaries of post-war government policies that gave a university education free of charge to well-qualified students irrespective of

[66] See, for instance, W. J. Arkell, *Oxford Stone* (London 1947), pp. 105–6.
[67] A. Clifton-Taylor, *The Pattern of English Building* (London 1972), p. 68; A. Clifton-Taylor and A. S. Ireson, *English Stone Building* (London 1983), pp. 107–8.
[68] e.g. at Brasenose and the Blue Boar quad at Christ Church.
[69] Chablo, 'University Architecture' p. 148.
[70] 20 Apr 1960.
[71] *Architects' Journal*, (17 Nov 1960), p. 729 The writer also criticized the spikes on top of the 'clerestory' towers and the external staircase leading from the North Quad to the central staircase hall.
[72] 17 Oct 1960.

28 One of the top-floor rooms in the Beehive, soon after completion

29 A drawing of a room in the Beehive (Architects' Co-Partnership)

their social background. In building the Beehive St John's catered for their physical needs in an exemplary manner.

The Beehive went up at the beginning of what turned out to be a huge expansion of building which changed the face of British universities.[73] Not long after its completion large new colleges were begun in both of the ancient universities—Churchill, New Hall, and Fitzwilliam in Cambridge, and St Catherine's in Oxford—and few of the older colleges remained unaffected by the new building mania. Even larger projects were undertaken in the redbrick universities. The Beehive was smaller and less ambitious than many of these schemes, and this may help to account for its success. It was well-built, and it has stood the test of time well. Opinions will always differ as to the wisdom or desirability of building in a 'contemporary' style within a historic context. But, with the Beehive, St John's rose to the challenge of commissioning a modernist design which respected the scale of an Oxford college while adding a distinctive aesthetic character peculiar to the mid-twentieth century. In doing so it pointed the way towards the subsequent transformation not only of the college but of Oxford as a whole.

[73] See M. Girouard, 'The English University of the Future', *Country Life Annual* (1961), pp. 22–4.

3 Vertebrate Architecture: the Sir Thomas White Building

The Sir Thomas White Building changed the character of St John's more than any building since the Canterbury Quadrangle in the 1630s. And, like the Canterbury Quadrangle, it expresses the ideals and aspirations of its time. Its genesis took place in the 1960s: a decade of unparalleled growth in university education in England. Despite post-war expansion, only 4 per cent of British 18-year-olds went to university in 1960.[1] In the ensuing decade growth was fuelled by the rising expectations of the post-war 'baby boom' generation of children nurtured by the Welfare State and by government demands for a trained scientific and techno-cratic elite capable of maintaining Britain's economic position in an increasingly competitive world. These demands were clearly articulated in the Robbins Report on university education of 1963, and, in a famous speech at the Labour Party conference of the same year, the future Prime Minister Harold Wilson exhorted his listeners to embrace his vision of the 'white heat' of the scientific revolution.[2]

The Robbins Report was an important step towards the modern concept of higher education as a right for the many rather than a privilege for the few. Its aims were unashamedly meritocratic. Higher education courses, it said, should be 'available to all those who are qualified by ability and attainment to pursue them and who wish to do so'. Local Education Authorities had already in 1962 undertaken to pay British students' tuition fees, and there were also generous maintenance grants. With financial inducements of this magnitude on offer, the number of students at British universities doubled from 113,000 in 1961 to 272,000 in 1977.[3] Much of the expansion occurred in the long-established redbrick universities, in the seven new universities founded between 1957 and 1961, and in a second wave of new foundations (many of them former technical colleges) that followed the Robbins Report. But there was also substantial, though less rapid, growth in Oxford and Cambridge. This was especially true of post-graduate students; Oxford's graduate student population went up by 40 per cent during the 1960s, and by the middle of the decade they already comprised 23 per cent of the student body , many of them coming from abroad.[4] Meanwhile, as a

---

[1] R. Stevens, *University to Uni* (London 2004), pp. 13–14. This figure does not include students at vocational and teacher training colleges.

[2] M. Sanderson, 'Social Equity and Industrial Need: a Dilemma of English Education since 1945', in T. Gourvish and A. O'Day (eds), *Britain Since 1945* (Basingstoke & London 1991), pp. 170–2; B. Pimlott, *Harold Wilson* (London 1992), p. 304.

[3] Stevens, *University to Uni*, pp. 26–35; S. Muthesius, *The Post-War University: Utopianist Campus and College* (New Haven and London 2001), p. 95; D. Chablo, 'University Architecture', pp. 1, 5, 64.

[4] K.V. Thomas, 'College Life 1945–1970' in Harrison (ed), *History of Oxford University: the Twentieth Century*, p. 210. The total number of students in Oxford grew from 7396 in 1958–9 to over 11,000 by the early 1970s.

result of the Hardie Report of 1962, a 'wholly meritocratic' system of under-graduate selection was adopted, leading to an increase in the proportion of students educated at grammar schools.[5] These developments profoundly changed the social character of the university.

During the 1960s university building became one of the most active and creative areas of architectural endeavour in Britain. As an editorial in the *Architectural Review* enthused in 1963:

A new and dynamic generation of younger dons, called to positions of command by the needs of the new universities being built, and by the normal process of staff turnover in the older universities being extended and improved, has given a new intellectual tone to university patronage ... The air of ivy-girt traditionalism has blown away. The aim now ... is to make universities contribute visibly to the progressive aspirations of the nation.[6]

By the mid-1960s this aim had borne fruit in Oxford: in new University buildings, such as Leslie Martin's monumental St Cross Building (1961–4) for the English, Law, and Economics faculties; in new colleges, notably Arne Jacobsen's St. Catherine's (1960–4), as bold a challenge to traditional ideas of collegiate architecture as Keble College had been a century earlier; in new blocks of rooms in the older colleges; even in ancillary buildings such as the elegant new St John's boathouse put up to the designs of Bridgewater and Shepheard, architects of the new University of Lancaster, in 1962–3.[7] Modernism was now the architectural lingua franca in Oxford, as it was elsewhere in Britain. It was a language that was sometimes spoken in harsh and guttural tones. Some architects, such as Jacobsen, adopted a restrained functionalist style characterized by unbroken lines and smooth surfaces, inspired by the work of Mies van der Rohe. But others aimed for a more expressive effect, often through the use of rough concrete, asymmetrical planning, and jagged and broken outlines. They looked back to the late, post-war work of Le Corbusier, whose buildings at Marseilles, Ronchamp, La Tourette, and Chandigarh prompted the cry of the 'New Brutalists' of the mid-1950s: 'Mies is great but Corb communicates.'[8] The search for an architecture which was at once functionalist and expressive continued throughout the 1960s and early 1970s, and it left its mark not just in Oxford and other universities but in towns and cities throughout Britain.

Despite the completion of the Beehive Building, St John's faced a growing shortage of housing space in the mid-1960s, due largely an expansion in the number of graduate students, of whom there were 128 by 1970: 98 more than in 1960.[9] The number of Fellows was increasing too. There were twenty-two in 1953, and during the 1960s new fellowships were established in chemistry,

[5] Harrison (ed), *History of Oxford University: the Twentieth Century*, p. 194.
[6] *Architectural Review* 134 (Oct. 1963), pp. 131–2.
[7] D. Chablo, 'Architecture', in B. Harrison (ed), *History of Oxford University: the Twentieth Century*, pp. 509–16; Tyack, *Oxford: An Architectural Guide*, pp. 304, 307–11. For the boathouse, see SJCA, Mun. lxxxi. 201.
[8] Jackson, *The Politics of Architecture*, p. 183. See also See R. Banham, *The New Brutalism* (London 1966), *passim*.
[9] *College Record* (1960, 1965, 1969–70).

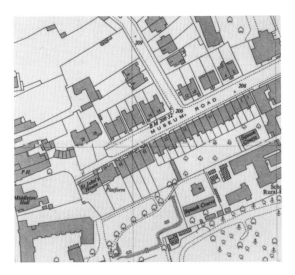

30 Plan of Museum Road, Blackhall Road, and the site of the Sir Thomas White Building

31 The President's vegetable garden and the backs of 33–9 Museum Road 1964. The Sir Thomas White Building stands on this site (Architects' Co-Partnership)

anatomy, engineering, psychology and modern languages. Undergraduates still had to spend their third year (or third and fourth years) in the dwindling supply of rented accommodation outside college.[10] So the college was forced to contemplate building again, and on a larger scale than before.

The obvious site for expansion was to the north of the North Quadrangle (Fig. 30). Here, behind the wall of the college garden, was the President's vegetable garden (Fig. 31) and, next to it, the college's Squash Courts. Further north was Museum Road, a throughfare that took its name from the University Museum of 1855 at its eastern end. Museum Road was lined on its south side by stuccoed terraced houses built on land belonging to Lincoln College in about 1840; the westernmost of these houses (numbers 25–31) were bought by St John's in 1965-6 and turned into postgraduate accommodation.[11] The semi-detached brick houses opposite (numbers 14–24) were put up in 1873 by the builder John Dorn on ground belonging to St John's (Fig. 32); they were turned over to the use of graduate students during the 1960s, along with another semi-detached pair of houses of 1873–5 in Blackhall Road, which ran north between the garden of the seventeenth-century Black Hall and Keble College, founded in 1868. At the western end of Museum Road was a somewhat charmless group of brick houses (numbers 33–9) put up in 1899 on St John's land by the local building firm of T. H. Kingerlee, and beyond were two houses put up by the college for tutors in 1898, one of which (Mansel House) was converted in 1961 into a rather dingy Middle Common Room for graduate students; the other (St John's House) had been used

[10] SJCA, Mun. lxxxi. 179(a).
[11] T. Hinchcliffe, *North Oxford*, pp. 192–3. See Fig. 63, p. 77.

32 The west end of Museum Road, looking west c.1964. On the left are numbers 33–9 and Mansel House, demolished to make way for the Sir Thomas White Building, with Middleton Hall beyond. The houses on the right (numbers 14–24) would also have been demolished under the original scheme for the development of the site (Architects' Co-Partnership)

since the 1950s as the Bursary.[12] A little further on, on the north side of a passageway leading past the Lamb and Flag inn to St Giles, was a blandly suburban-looking pair of semi-detached brick houses for college tutors, put up to the designs of Sir Edward Maufe in 1938. These buildings were all hidden from public view by a row of college-owned houses flanking St Giles, stretching north from Middleton Hall past the Lamb and Flag and the handsome detached stone house of 1702 now known as St Giles House[13] as far as Black Hall, leased to Queen Elizabeth House, which put up its own premises alongside it in 1961.[14]

The origins of what became the Sir Thomas White Building go back to 1964, when the Bursar, Arthur Garrard, drew up a plan for putting up new buildings for both graduates and undergraduates on the college-owned property at the western end of Museum Road, with the postgraduates housed on the northern part of the site and the undergraduates to the south.[15] Expansion on this site would enable the college to house another 120 students in addition to the 153 already housed in college without the need for purchasing any land.[16] The Victorian houses in what was already being described as a 'graduate colony'[17] would have to be demolished, but the conservation lobby was not yet strong or vociferous enough to fight for

[12] Ibid, pp. 51, 112, 166, 220, 232.

[13] Since 1852 it had been leased to the County to accommodate the itinerant judges on assize, and was known as the Judge's Lodgings. It was taken over by the college and turned to its own uses after 1964: SJCA, ADM I.A.12, p. 143.

[14] See pp. 118–9.

[15] SJCA, Mun lxxxi.170, 20 Apr. 1964.

[16] In 1960 there were 67 bed-sitting rooms, 78 two-room sets, and 4 double sets (two bedrooms and a shared sitting-room) in college, including Middleton Hall. There were also 26 fellows' rooms and three sets for resident fellows.

[17] College Record (1965).

them. Garrard was conscious that building on this scale would change the physical and even the social character of what was still during the 1960s a relatively close-knit and introspective community. But times were changing and he told the Estates Committee in 1964 that '[the] College should no longer be thought of as a collection of buildings within a *cheval-de-frise*-topped wall, but less monastically, as containing a mixed community with houses for tutors, accommodation for married and single graduates with their social centre, college administrative offices, etc':[18] a perceptive assessment of the way in which both the character and the appearance of Oxford colleges would, in time, evolve.

Nothing was done about Garrard's proposals until 1966, when the Graduate Facilities Committee of the Governing Body asked for an architect's appraisal of the site.[19] A New Building Committee was then set up, with Howard Colvin, by now a member of the Royal Fine Arts Commission, as one of its members.[20] In October it recommended approaching three firms of architects: the Architects' Co-Partnership, William Whitfield, and Powell and Moya.[21] All had made their mark in university building. Michael Powers of the Architects' Co-Partnership had followed his widely acclaimed success in the St John's Beehive by designing an inconspicuous but spatially inventive pair of detached and semi-detached houses for tutors and their families on the western side of Blackhall Road in 1962–3 (Figs. 33–4).[22] The firm had also worked for the University of Durham, where their Dunelm House (1961–5), incorporating the students' union, exploits the dramatic potential of the site on the banks of the River Wear, and in 1963 one of the partners, Kenneth Capon, was chosen as architect for the new University of Essex.[23] Whitfield had designed nothing in Oxford, but he was responsible for university buildings at Durham (the Science Library of 1963–6), Newcastle (the students' union, refectory, and debating chamber, 1960–4), and, most important-ly, at Glasgow, where he designed an impressive library (1965–8) flanked by service towers, followed later by an art gallery extension that ingeniously incorporated Charles Rennie Mackintosh's house.[24] The best-known of the three firms was that of Philip Powell and Hidalgo Moya. Favoured by Colvin for their 'exceptionally high professional standards', they had made their reputations with the famous Churchill Gardens housing estate at Pimlico (1947–52)—one of the

[18] SJCA, Mun lxxxi.170, 20 Apr 1964. A *cheval-de-frise* is a spiked horizontal iron pole at the top of a wall.
[19] SJCA, ADM I.A.12, p. 202; Mun. lxxxi. 170, 9 Feb 1966.
[20] SJCA, ADM I.A.12, p. 220. The other members were the President, J. D. Mabbott; Arthur Garrard; the Domestic Bursar; the chaplain, Eric Heaton (later to become Dean of Christ Church); a modern linguist, T. J. Reed; and a physicist, Roger Elliott. Reed later resigned, and the original members were joined by the historian, Keith Thomas, the English Literature tutor John Carey, and A. F. Martin, a geographer.
[21] SJCA, ADM I.A.12, p. 223; Mun. lxxxi. 170, 9 June, 5 Oct 1966,.
[22] *Architects' Journal* (26 June 1963), pp. 1347–56; E. Harwood, *England: a Guide to Post-War Buildings,* rev edn (London 2003).
[23] N. Pevsner and E. Williamson, *The Buildings of England: County Durham* (Harmondsworth 1983), pp. 233–4; Muthesius, *The Post-War University,* pp. 153–7.
[24] N. Pevsner and I. Richmond, *The Buildings of England: Northumberland* (2nd edn London 1992), pp. 449–50; Pevsner & Williamson, *The Buildings of England: County Durham,* p. 235. E. Williamson, A. Riches and M. Higgs, *The Buildings of Scotland: Glasgow* (London 1990), p. 344.

33 The tutors' houses in Blackhall Road (1962–3) (Architects' Co-Partnership)

34 The interior of one of the Blackhall Road tutors' houses

pioneering examples of post-war modernist architecture—and the Skylon at the Festival of Britain. In the late 1950s and early 60s they became one of the most widely employed architectural practices in Oxford and Cambridge, designing a series of buildings which succeeded in marrying modernist aesthetics with a widely-praised sensitivity to the *genius loci*.[25]

In the end none of these firms was chosen. Powell and Moya, a small practice of only fifteen people whose hands were full with existing commissions—including one for a new graduate college (Wolfson College) built on land sold by St John's in North Oxford—declined to compete, and two more firms entered the lists in their place.[26] Howell, Killick, Partridge and Amis first achieved prominence in the 1950s as architects of the Alton West housing estate at Roehampton in south-west London for the London County Council (1954–8)—Britain's answer to Le Corbusier's Unité d'Habitation at Marseilles—and were strongly associated with the 'New Brutalist' avant-garde of the Smithsons and of Team X, the self-consciously experimental grouping that emerged out of the tenth and last CIAM (Congrès Internationaux d'Architecture Moderne) meeting in 1956. They went on to build up a large university practice: at Birmingham (Department of Commerce and Social Science, completed 1964); at Cambridge—the Graduate Centre (1964–7), and work at Darwin College (1966–8) and at Sidney Sussex, sister college of St John's (1967–9);[27] and in Oxford, where they were responsible for the expansion of St Anne's College (1966–9), and for the sinister but compelling hall and common room at St Antony's, conceived as part of a much larger plan in 1960, but not built until 1968–70.[28]

The fourth of the competing firms, Arup Associates, came into being in 1963 as a partnership between the engineer Ove Arup—one of the crucial figures in the early years of modernist architecture in England in the 1930s—and the architect Philip Dowson (Fig. 35). Dowson, who took charge of the St John's project from the beginning, was born in South Africa, read Fine Arts at Cambridge, and attended the Architectural Association school from 1950 to 1953.[29] He then joined the firm of Ove Arup and Partners—consultant engineers for the Architects' Co-Partnership's Brynmawr Rubber Factory—and developed an overtly functionalist style in a high-rise block of flats, Point Royal, at Bracknell New Town (1959–64) and, later, in a series of collegiate buildings including the Vaughan and Fry block for Somerville College in Little Clarendon Street, Oxford (Fig. 36)—commissioned in the same year as the Beehive but not built until 1962–4[30]—and a

35 Sir Philip Dowson (Sir Philip Dowson)

[25] e.g. Brasenose, Christ Church and Corpus Christi, Oxford; the Cripps Building at St John's, Cambridge.
[26] Other architects considered and rejected were Denys Lasdun, Alison and Peter Smithson, Maguire and Murray, and Gollins, Melville and Ward.
[27] P. Booth and Nicholas Taylor, *Cambridge New Architecture* (London 1970), pp. 47–8, 62–3, 149–50.
[28] S. Cantacuzino, *Howell, Killick, Partridge and Amis: Architecture* (London 1981), pp. 29. 32–40. See also Chablo, 'University Architecture', pp. 84, 187–90.
[29] A. L. Morgan and C. Naylor (eds) *Contemporary Architects* (Chicago & London 1987) p. 241; M. Brawne, *Arup Associates* (London 1983), pp. 14-15.
[30] P. Adams, *Somerville for Women* (Oxford 1996), pp. 273–5.

36 The Vaughan/Fry Building for Somerville College (1962–4) in Little Clarendon Street, Oxford, designed by Philip Dowson of Arup Associates. (Thomas Photos, © Oxfordshire County Council Photographic Archive)

highly-praised graduate block for Corpus Christi College, Cambridge in the garden of Leckhampton House, Grange Road (also 1962–4). He was also responsible for the Department of Metallurgy and Mining at the University of Birmingham (1962–4) and for two other large complexes of laboratories and ancillary buildings which were not finished until the early 1970s: Oxford's Department of Nuclear Physics at the southern end of the 'Keble Road triangle', best known for its extraordinary fan-shaped concrete linear accelerator tower, and the New Museums site between Downing Street and Lion Yard in Cambridge. These buildings all display a rigorous structural logic and proclaim an interest in the architectural potential of concrete and glass: qualities that immediately strike any visitor to the Sir Thomas White Building.

Arup Associates prided itself on its 'scientific' approach to architecture, based on that pioneered in the Bauhaus at Dessau, Germany, during the 1920s.[31] For its

[31] Brawne, *Arup Associates*, p. 29.

members, as for Hannes Meyer, Walter Gropius's successor as head of the Bauhaus, building was 'no longer an individual task for the realization of architectural ambitions. Building is the communal effort of craftsmen and inventors . . . Building is nothing but organization: social, technical, economic, psychological organization'.[32] That belief was echoed by Dowson, who thought that 'close-knit, interdisciplinary design teams are necessary to confront the scale and complexity of modern buildings.'[33] By 1983 the firm was made up of four architects, three structural engineers, two service engineers and two quantity surveyors, ensuring that a large project could, at least in theory, be conceived and executed collaboratively, without any need to bring in external professional expertise.

The first instructions prepared by the college in 1966 were very ambitious. Not only would there be accommodation—both bed-sitting rooms and two-roomed sets—for 30 married and 90 unmarried students, mainly postgraduates but also some third-year undergraduates who needed housing in college because of what the College Record called 'the progressive decline in lodgings'.[34] There would also be a house and two flats for Fellows, a lecture room accommodating 160 people, a new Middle Common Room for the graduate students, a science library designed to cater for an anticipated threefold expansion in the number of books over the next twenty-five years,[35] and parking, possibly underground, for a hundred cars. Work was expected to begin in 1969, and to take three years. Early in 1967 the college invited the four chosen firms to enter a limited competition for a new appraisal—more detailed than a development plan but less than a fully-fledged design—to be submitted by May 1967, with a prize of £2500 for the winner. By now the brief had been expanded to include a dining room for a hundred people, next to the Middle Common Room, and a porter's lodge; an indoor swimming pool was also mentioned as desirable but not essential. The cost was to be between £400,000 and £600,000, and work was to start in 1970.[36]

The four sets of designs submitted to the college in Trinity term 1967 shared a common approach to collegiate planning and architecture.[37] In each the traditional enclosed quadrangular model was loosened in favour of irregular groupings of blocks, sometimes in open-ended courtyards. This way of laying out a building drew its inspiration from some of the pioneering structures of the 1920s, above all the Bauhaus building at Dessau in Germany. It was employed in several American universities, such as the Harvard Graduate Center designed by Walter Gropius, architect of the Bauhaus, in 1949,[38] and it also appears in some English educational institutions of the late 1950s and early 1960s, notably in Richard Sheppard,

[32] U. Conrads (ed.), Programs and Manifestoes on Modern Architecture (Cambridge, Mass., 1970), p. 120.
[33] Contemporary Architects, p. 243.
[34] SJCA, ADM I.A.12, p. 202; Mun. lxxxi. 170; College Record (1967).
[35] SJCA, Mun. lxxxi. 170, 4 Mar 1966.
[36] SJCA, Mun. lxxxi. 170, 2 Jan, 6 Feb 1967.
[37] Models of each firm's designs are preserved in the Muniment Room, together with sets of plans, some of them uncatalogued.
[38] P. V. Turner, Campus: an American Planning Tradition (Cambridge, Mass., and London 1984), pp. 267–8.

Robson and Partners' Churchill College, Cambridge (1961–8), where it was impressively combined with an architectural language of elemental forms expressed in bare brick and rough concrete, derived from the later work of Le Corbusier.[39]

The Architects' Co-Partnership proposed a four-phase development of the site, starting with an open courtyard on the site of the Museum Road and Blackhall Road houses, linked by a bridge over Museum Road to separate blocks to the south and west (Fig. 37). Howell, Killick, Partridge and Amis planned to put a massive three-sided east-facing courtyard between Museum Road and the college garden (roughly on the site of the present Sir Thomas White building) and a smaller L-shaped block on the site of the houses in Museum Road and Blackhall Road (Fig. 38). The external treatment, which Colvin dismissed as 'crude and repetitious', would have been like that of the Cambridge Graduate Centre and their buildings at St Anne's College, Oxford, with splayed windows bulging out of a concrete frame. Whitfield also wanted to put most of the buildings on the southern part of the site. They would be grouped around a courtyard over a subterranean car park, with a massive square tower on the western side, described by Colvin as a 'granite citadel or Norman keep'; a smaller rectangular block would have gone at a later stage on the site of the houses on the northern side of Museum Road, linked to the southern buildings by a footbridge (Fig. 39).[40] But it was the design by Philip Dowson of Arup Associates that appealed most to the New Building Committee, and he was selected as architect by the Governing Body *nem. con.* in June 1967.[41]

The controlling idea behind Dowson's plan was that of circulation. The buildings would be arranged in a broadly linear fashion (Fig. 40), as in the unexecuted but influential plan prepared by the Smithsons for the University of Sheffield in 1953,[42] and in Powell and Moya's design for the Cripps Building at St John's College, Cambridge (1963–8)—one of the best collegiate projects of the 1960s. Dowson was impressed by the 'sense of calm derived from the relationship between the gardens and the quiet formality of the main buildings [at St John's] . . . When walking though St John's one moves through a series of related spaces. Any new development must, in our view, draw from this principle, revealing itself in a gradual fashion'.[43] A series of connected pavilions containing study-bedrooms would be arranged in an irregular line leading north from the college garden to the new library, lecture room, and Middle Common Room on the south side of Museum Road. From here another range of buildings would stretch north, overlooking an open space created out of the gardens of the Victorian houses on the

[39] Muthesius, *The Post-War University*, pp. 65–8.
[40] Each firm's reports are in SJCA, Mun. lxxxi. 170, as are Colvin's handwritten, and undated, comments. The models are preserved in the Muniment Room.
[41] SJCA, ADM I.A.12, p. 256.
[42] Chablo, 'University Architecture', p. 83; Muthesius, op.cit., p. 62.
[43] SJCA, Mun. lxxxi. 178(a); Mun. lxxxi. 170.

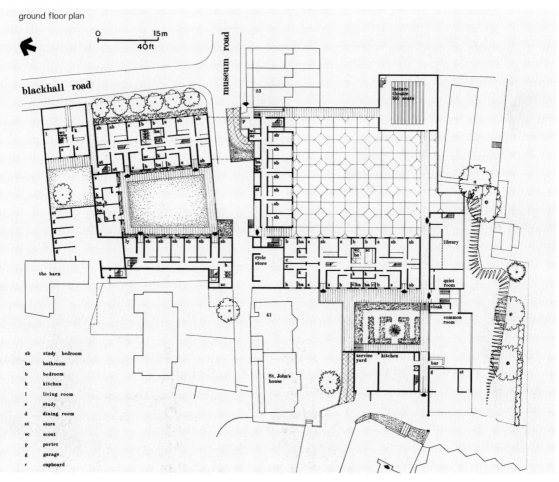

ground floor plan

blackhall road

museum road

leisure theatre
160 seats

23

the barn

41

cycle store

library

quiet room

cloak

common room

service yard   kitchen

bar

St. John's house

sb	study bedroom
ba	bathroom
b	bedroom
k	kitchen
l	living room
s	study
d	dining room
st	store
sc	scout
p	porter
g	garage
c	cupboard

37 Plan by the Architects' Co-Partnership showing the proposed treatment of the Museum Road site (north is to the left) (Architects' Co-Partnership)

38 A model of the design for the Museum Road site by Howell Killick, Partridge and Amis, looking north with the college garden in front

39 A model of the design for the Museum Road site by William Whitfield. The North Quadrangle is to the left

40 A schematic diagram (1967) showing Arup Associates' proposed treatment of the Museum Road site

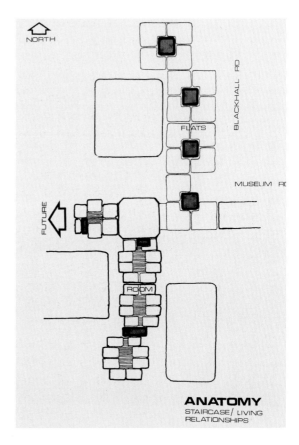

41 Arup Associates' first scheme for the Museum Road site (1967), first-floor plan. North is to the left and the north-east corner of the North Quadrangle at the bottom right. The proposed new lecture room is at the centre of the development (no. 5 on the plan)

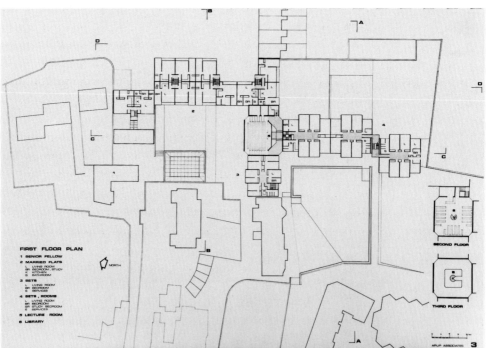

north side of Museum Road and the west side of Blackhall Road (Fig. 41). Though Dowson had little to say about architectural treatment, he assured the college that the buildings would 'exploit the natural assets of the site', and that a 'monumental' effect would be avoided. With this in mind, the Governing Body gave a hostage to fortune when it agreed on 29 July 1967 to 'leave Mr Dowson a free hand in designing the building and to confine our requirements to practical problems arising from the use of the area'.[44] Dowson was, however, asked to give special attention to the relationship of the southern block to the college garden and to avoid the use of rough-faced concrete and excessive amounts of glass: provisos that he interpreted with some latitude.

Before Dowson could proceed to making detailed plans the college still had to clarify what it wanted from the new buildings, and how it was to pay for them. The guidelines given to the competing architects early in 1967 were conceived in an expansionary frame of mind. But, with inflation rising, second thoughts began to surface, prompted by a report undertaken in December 1967 by the new Bursar, Harry Kidd, an old member of the college who had been Secretary of the London School of Economics. He estimated that the complete project would cost £1,150,000, if inflation were taken into account, not the £700,000 originally estimated, and on 17 January 1968 the New Building Committee was asked to re-examine Dowson's scheme, especially with a view to the kitchens, library and the phasing of the project.[45] This led to significant alterations to the brief. The swimming pool—never seen as a major priority—was dropped in April 1968.[46] The science library was also sacrificed, and a decision was taken later to create a new library for 50,000 books (the present Lower Library) out of five sets of comfortable, and newly refurbished, rooms under the Old Library in the Canterbury Quadrangle.[47] This work was conceived and planned by Howard Colvin, as Librarian, in collaboration with Walter Price of the Oxford Architects' Partnership, and was carried out in 1975–6, after the completion of the Sir Thomas White Building.[48] Yet while some items were subtracted from the brief, others were being added. The most important was a 'chapter house' for Governing Body meetings, intended to relieve pressure on the Senior Common Room: a perennial source of concern as the fellowship expanded during the 1960s and 1970s.[49] This room could, it was argued, go in the space originally designated for the science library over the lecture room.[50] Following consultations with the graduate students, it was also decided to increase the number of two-room sets:[51] a recommendation that was bound to lead to a considerable increase in cost.

[44] SJCA, ADM I.A.12, p. 260.
[45] SJCA, Mun. lxxxi. 170, 5 Dec 1967; ADM I.A.12, pp. 278, 282–3.
[46] SJCA, ADM I.A.12, p. 298.
[47] Colvin, Canterbury Quadrangle, p. 91.
[48] SJCA, ADM I.A.12, pp. . 294, 403; Mun. lxxxi. 170, 8 Feb 13, 14 Mar 1968. Information from Sir Howard Colvin.
[49] See pp. 000–000.
[50] SJCA, Mun. lxxxi. 170, 13 Jan 1969.
[51] SJCA, Mun. lxxxi. 170, 27 Nov 1967.

The changes to the brief took place at a time when the college was embarking on a major review of its finances, necessitated initially by the passing of a long-anticipated Leasehold Reform Act by Harold Wilson's government in 1967.[52] Dismissed in 1969 by Hugh Trevor-Roper ('Mercurius Oxoniensis') as 'a dull place north of Balliol, but monstrous rich',[53] St John's in the late 1960s possessed assets worth some £9,000,000, two-thirds of which were still locked up in real estate, comprising 9000 acres of agricultural land as well as the North Oxford estate.[54] By now many of the North Oxford houses were nearly 100 years old, with 24 of the original 99-year leases due to expire in 1970 and another 36 by 1973. For Harry Kidd the impending sale of the remaining houses through leasehold enfranchisement represented not so much a threat as an opportunity. Oxford University was clamouring for accommodation for its own rapidly proliferating departments, and other institutions were equally desperate for space. First conceived as a suburban *rus in urbe*, North Oxford could be gradually infiltrated by academe.

In June 1968 the Governing Body authorized a 'substantial reduction' of the college's holdings of residential property. The proceeds of the sales were initially to be devoted to funding the new buildings, leaving, after their completion, half of the assets in stock exchange investments and half in a real property portfolio 'much more diversified than at present, residential and agricultural property forming a smaller part and good freehold, commercial and industrial property forming a larger part of it'.[55] The passing of the Universities and Colleges Estates Act (1964) had removed earlier restrictions on the college's management of its endowment income, and a series of sales followed during the later 1960s and 1970s, not only in North Oxford but also in the Berkshire and Oxfordshire villages where St John's had owned property for many generations.[56] Finally, in 1971, the college resolved to sell the remainder of its agricultural estate, save only for that at Fyfield (Berkshire, now Oxfordshire), where Sir Thomas White, the founder of the college, had established his family.[57] This decision was never fully acted upon, and the college subsequently bought more agricultural land,[58] but St John's nevertheless became increasingly dependent on the potentially more lucrative income from commercial property and equities. It could therefore embark on its building plans without recourse to outside funding or appeals to old members, while at the same time building up its academic reputation by expanding its teaching and research capacity.

But the sale of property on the scale envisaged was bound to take a long time, and in the short term funds were limited. Dowson had already made clear that his

---

[52] SJCA, ADM I.A.12, p. 277. See J. Dunbabin, 'Finance since 1914' in Harrison (ed), *History of the University of Oxford: the Twentieth Century*, p. 668.
[53] [H. R. Trevor-Roper], *The Letters of Mercurius* (London 1970), p. 32.
[54] *College Record* (1973–4).
[55] SJCA, ADM I.A.12, pp. 313, 326.
[56] Hinchcliffe, *North Oxford*, pp. 196, 202–6.
[57] SJCA, Mun. lxxxi. 170, 19 Feb, 3 Mar 1970; ADM. I.A.13, p. 33.
[58] It currently (2004) owns about 6000 acres.

scheme could be built in two stages, and in January 1968 the Governing Body decided to build half of it by 1972, the rest following in the ensuing decade.[59] In April 1968 Kidd proposed that work should start on the southern part of the site, and to set aside £490,000 for the purpose: a sum that was later increased to £600,000 as the result of a decision to face the buildings in stone.[60] The money was to be earmarked from the proceeds of the sale of the sixty North Oxford houses whose leases were due to expire by 1973.[61] With funding secured, Dowson could now produce a definitive design for the southern part of the site, which he submitted in January 1969. This provided 45 two-roomed sets, 45 bed-sitting rooms—as opposed to the 60 study-bedrooms and 30 sets originally envisaged—and four flats for married graduates, as well as a lecture room, a dining room, a Middle Common Room and parking for 70 cars. The scheme was revised a month later to incorporate the 'chapter house', and, following further refinements in May 1969,[62] the design was submitted to the college in October 1969.[63]

Dowson's final scheme did not depart in its essentials from the plan that had won the approval of the college in 1967, except for the omission of the northern portion, which it was still assumed would follow later. The four-storeyed building was to be constructed around a pre-cast concrete frame, visible externally, with concrete floors and staircases and services in the central spine of each block. It would be laid out in the shape of the letter T over an underground car park, with one range of buildings facing Museum Road and another projecting south, the southern end of which would take the form of a slightly higher tower overlooking the college garden; a new, detached block of squash courts would be placed in a separate building to the east. The lecture room was to go at the centre of the frontage to Museum Road, with the 'chapter house' cantilevered out above it and a reception area and a new porter's lodge below (Fig. 42). It would be flanked to the east by the kitchens and dining room and to the west by a residential block with an overhanging top floor (Fig. 43), as in Rudolph Schindler's famous Lovell Beach House at Newport Beach, California (1925–6), one of the pioneering works of American modernism, and, more recently, Dowson's own New Museums development in Cambridge.[64]

Most of the accommodation was to be placed in the north–south block, two rooms deep, with the Middle Common Room behind an open 'cloister' on the ground floor, and a bar in the block at the southern end, which was to be skewed slightly to the west of the main axis. The bed-sitting rooms would go on the first

[59] SJCA, ADM I.A.12, pp. 282–3.
[60] SJCA, Mun. lxxxi. 170, 4 Apr, 18 Sept 1968.
[61] SJCA, Mun. lxxxi. 170, 5 Dec. 1967. In the end the college spent in the region of £1,500,000 on a building only half the size of that originally intended, though containing a substantial proportion of the residential accommodation.
[62] SJCA, Mun. lxxxi.178.e.
[63] SJCA, Mun. lxxxi.178.f.
[64] The model (Fig. 43) is preserved in the Muniment Room.

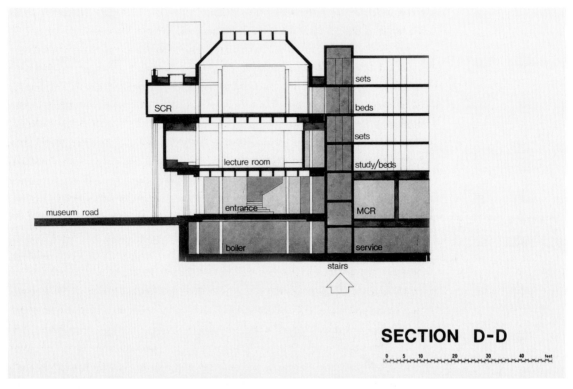

SECTION D-D

0 5 10 20 30 40 feet

42 A cross-section of the Museum Road frontage in the revised design (1969), showing the 'chapter house' for the senior members of the college on the top floor

43 A model of the proposed Museum Road façade (1969), with the lecture room and 'chapter house' block in the centre and residential accommodation to the right

floor, with the two-roomed sets on the three floors above, their bedrooms, occupying the third floor, cunningly sandwiched between the sitting rooms on the second and fourth floors, and linked to them by spiral staircases in the central core: an arrangement also seen in buildings at the Universities of Leeds and Surrey.[65] The study-bedrooms and the sitting rooms of the sets would be generously planned on the basis of 200 square feet per room—the same as the Beehive rooms, and much larger than the University Grants Committee norm of 100–140 square feet. And at £2370 per room and £3260 per set, they would cost more than twice or, in the case of the sets, more than three times, the sum recommended by the UGC.[66]

In Michaelmas term 1969 the medieval historian Sir Richard Southern replaced J. D. Mabbott as President. His arrival coincided with, and perhaps helped precipitate, a major reconsideration of Dowson's plans. An Oxford college is governed by its Fellows, and the head of house is a *primus inter pares*, not an all-powerful figure like the vice-chancellor of a new university. But, at least as far as building was concerned, Southern took a more dynamic view of his role than his immediate predecessors, who were in general content to leave decisions to the Building Committees appointed by the Governing Body. Dowson's plans came under increasing scrutiny partly, but not entirely, for financial reasons. By the autumn of 1969 the estimated cost of the whole project, including the portion to the north of Museum Road, had risen to £1,700,000—well over double the estimate of 1967.[67] Yet the new buildings on the southern site would give a net increase of accommodation for only sixty-seven students if the loss of the rooms in 25–39 Museum Road were taken into account, and more demolition of houses currently used to accommodate postgraduates would be necessary if the northern part of the scheme were ever to be built. Harry Kidd criticized Dowson for allowing 'an autogenous growth in size', especially noticeable in the Middle Common Room, which had grown from 1000 to 2675 square feet. Here, he lamented, 'the design seems to have taken charge of the architects rather than *vice versa*'.[68] But his colleagues did not escape censure either. They had changed their minds over the brief by agreeing to increase the number of two-roomed sets and by deciding to face the building in stone. Above all, the architects had been given no clear cost limits, and were apparently 'once or twice adjured at meetings of the New Buildings Committee not to spoil the ship for a ha'porth of tar'. One of the members of the Building Committee later blamed the Governing Body as a whole for 'blithely and expensively' changing its mind over the requirements.[69] Worried by the financial implications of proceeding with Dowson's scheme in its entirety, a special meeting of the Fellows was convened on 24 October 1969 at which it was

[65] Chablo, 'University Architecture', p. 149.
[66] SJCA, Mun. lxxxi. 170, 15 Sept 1969.
[67] SJCA, Mun. lxxxi. 179(a), 27 Jan 1970.
[68] SJCA, Mun. lxxxi. 170, 21 Oct 1969.
[69] SJCA, Mun. lxxxi. 179(a), 19 Jan 1970.

agreed to abandon the already postponed northern half. So the sturdily built Victorian houses on the northern side of Museum Road (numbers 14–24), and in Blackhall Road were saved.[70]

Dowson was 'very disappointed' by the proposed emasculation of what he described as his best ever design for Oxford or Cambridge, and he told Kidd that '[it] was very worrying that so much time, effort and money had been wasted on the preparation of a scheme based on a brief which was now itself to be changed'.[71] The southern part of the scheme, he asserted, could not stand alone, and it would be necessary to make a completely new design. This was already inevitable because the college had again changed its mind about its requirements. The original scheme had been driven by the need to house more postgraduates; now the decision was taken to increase the number of undergraduates. The Governing Body therefore decided in December 1970 to house the married graduate students in a new block called Hart-Synnot House to be erected behind college-owned houses at 99–111 Woodstock Road; the architect of this un-prepossessing structure, which went up in 1973–4, was Richard Gray of Pinkheard and Partners, the Beaumont Street firm that had taken over the practice of Booth and Lederboer, which had extended the Senior Common Room in the 1950s.[72] The Governing Body also resolved to abandon the 'chapter house' in the new building and to extend the existing Senior Common Room instead.[73] The need for a new lecture room had never been very clearly defined either, and in the new brief, prepared in February 1970, this too was abandoned.

Dowson now agreed to go back to the drawing board to design a 'self-contained entity' for both undergraduates and unmarried postgraduates on the southern part of the Museum Road site.[74] This was a very different project from the one he had originally expected to build. Shorn of most of its 'public' rooms, the building became a large and tightly planned range of student accommodation on the college's northern periphery. Kidd believed that 'the right way to get the best out of the architects is to ask them for rather more than can be provided for the sum that is available. The resulting squeeze should put them on their mettle.'[75] In practice this meant putting thirty more students than were envisaged in the original scheme on a site half the size. Half of the 150 or so students would live in sets, the rest in bed-sitting rooms.[76] As a first step towards working out the dimensions of the rooms, Kidd gathered information on comparable student residences at Somerville College and Trinity Hall, Cambridge (both by Dowson); at St John's

[70] SJCA, Mun. lxxxi. 170, 24 Oct 1969.
[71] SJCA, Mun. lxxxi. 179(a), 11 Nov 1969.
[72] SJCA, ADM I.A.13, p. 22; Mun. lxxxi. 175; *College Record* (1972–3, 1973–4). Extra accommodation for graduate students was supplied in Pusey Lane.
[73] SJCA, ADM I.A.12, pp. 383–4; Mun. lxxxi. 170, 5 Nov 1969. For the expansion of the Senior Common Room, see Appendix I.
[74] SJCA, Mun. lxxxi. 170, 24 Oct 1969; lxxxi. 179(a).
[75] SJCA, Mun. lxxxi. 179(a), 27 Jan, 10 Feb 1970.
[76] SJCA, Mun. lxxxi. 170, 10 Feb, 3 Mar 1970.

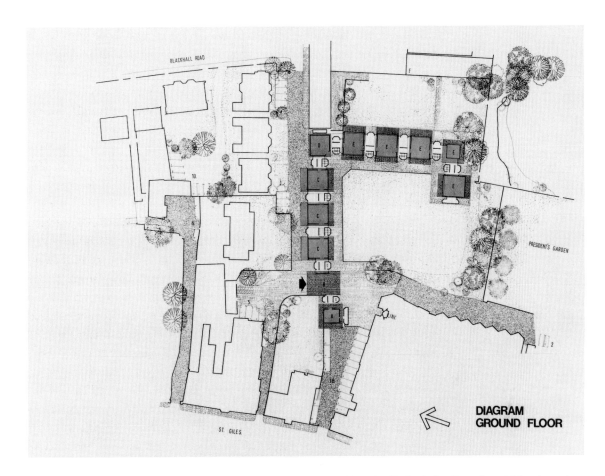

DIAGRAM
GROUND FLOOR

44 A block plan of the southern site (1970), showing the loose arrangement of pavilion blocks around the perimeter. North is to the left and the North Quadrangle at the bottom right

College, Cambridge, and Christ Church, Oxford (by Powell and Moya), and at Sidney Sussex, Cambridge, and St Anne's, Oxford (by Howell, Killick, Partridge and Amis).[77] The rooms would be of varied sizes, grouped around staircases. But, in a break with tradition, they would be serviced not by male scouts but by women cleaners: a decision that recognized a major social change of the late 1960s under which, in the words of a member of the New Building Committee, '[the Oxford] undergraduate was no longer a young gentleman with his personal servant; he had become the occupant of a hard-pressed and multi-purpose boarding house'.[78] The construction of the new building would not only enable the college to expand—from 371 in 1970 to 430 in 1980[79]; it would also, in a significant break with tradition, offer all undergraduates the prospect of three years' accommodation.

Dowson's ideas on the college's revised requirements were finally revealed in a feasibility study submitted October 1970 (Fig. 44). The enclosed character of the college would now be reinforced by creating a new courtyard beyond the North

[77] SJCA, Mun. lxxxi. 178(g).
[78] K.V. Thomas, in Harrison (ed), *History of Oxford University: the Twentieth Century*, p. 208.
[79] SJCA, Mun. lxxxi. 170, 27 Feb 1970.

Quadrangle, separated from the outside world by an L-shaped wall of residential buildings. Taking into account current interests in 'perimeter planning'—later seen in Gillespie, Kidd and Coia's Robinson College, Cambridge (1977–80)—they would be wrapped around the northern and eastern edges of the site, enclosing an open space looking south to the garden, with one block flanking Museum Road, the other stretching south to the garden wall, and the outer walls of the North Quadrangle at the south-western corner. The decision to place the buildings around the edge of the site changed the character of the project at a stroke, and enabled Dowson and his team to develop a design that would be at the same time functional and responsive to its surroundings.

Further changes to the brief soon followed. After consultations with the undergraduates, the Governing Body decided to remove the Junior Common Room from its comfortable club-like rooms at the south-east corner of the Front Quadrangle—one of which became the New Seminar Room—to the ground floor of the new building, where it would share some at least of the space with the Middle Common Room.[80] This raised the prospect of an undesirable social polarization between the new buildings, given over to junior members, and the older parts of the college. Partly in order to avert this, and partly to make more financial savings, the proposed new dining room was also abandoned, to be revived in a rather different guise when the Garden Quadrangle was built twenty years later.[81] The underground car park was sacrificed too. In the spacious days of the 1960s, with fewer and fewer Fellows living in college, and an increasing number colonizing the villages around Oxford's periphery, on-site car parking had been seen as an essential part of any new building. Now, with the environmental disadvantages of unlimited car travel becoming more and more obvious, these ideas were called into question, and a much more limited scheme for a car park for between thirty-five and forty cars on the President's drive, between the North Quadrangle and Middleton Hall, was proposed instead.

The new scheme entailed the demolition of several houses on the south side of Museum Road, though fewer than had been envisaged in Dowson's first plans. The Bursary was condemned, as was Mansel House, with the Middle Common Room —described by Southern as 'something of a licensed (in both senses of the word) bear-garden separate from the college'[82]—and the adjacent terrace of late-Victorian houses (nos. 33–9).[83] But without the need for access to an underground car park, the adjacent stuccoed houses (nos. 25–31) were spared and turned into student accommodation.[84] Expelled from St John's House, the Bursar took up residence in the north-east corner of the North Quadrangle, which now became the focal point of the college's administration.[85]

[80] SJCA, ADM I.A.13, p. 19.
[81] SJCA, ADM I.A.13, p. 37. Dowson was asked to prepare designs for a dining room over the kitchen in the Cook's Building in the North Quadrangle, but this proposal came to nothing.
[82] SJCA, Mun. lxxxi. 179(b), 21 Sept 1970.   [83] SJCA, Mun. lxxxi. 178(f).
[84] SJCA, Mun. lxxxi. 170, 14, 23, 28 Oct and 2 Nov 1970.
[85] SJCA, Mun. lxxxi. 170, 17 Feb 1971.

Writing after the completion of the Sir Thomas White Building, Dowson remarked that '[the] combination of the scale of this scheme and the complexity of its brief, with the extreme vulnerability of its site, presented the most difficult architectural problem we have ever had to undertake.'[86] The essence of the scheme is embodied in a set of diagrams and room plans finally submitted to the college, after extensive consultation, in June 1971.[87] They envisaged a series of eleven residential pavilions arranged like a 'string of beads': a concept employed in several university projects at the time, including Howell, Killick, Partridge and Amis's never-completed extensions to St Anne's College, Oxford.[88] They would be laid out on a slightly staggered plan and would be linked by narrower service blocks containing staircases, each of which would give access to four rooms per floor, with the ground floor devoted to the Junior and Middle Common Rooms, the precise relationship between which remained to be determined. The service blocks would be extended upwards as towers to allow a varied silhouette, and the open courtyard would be landscaped.[89] The eastern range, stretching towards the garden, was slightly skewed in order to preserve two trees, and its southern end was extended slightly to the west to impart a sense of enclosure to the new courtyard. Monotony was further avoided by making the pavilions at the ends of each range square in plan, rather than rectangular like the other pavilions. The cost was estimated at £1,374,500.

Dowson unveiled his final scheme in December 1971 (Figs 45–6).[90] By now relations between the college and the architect had now become somewhat strained, and Southern urged the New Buildings Committee to make up its mind about the remaining contentious issues, notably the height of the service towers, the deployment of tinted glass for the windows, and the use of stone cladding. As he said:

[We] have all the information now that we are ever likely to have until the building is put up. If we continue to negotiate we must expect Dowson to continue to press his point of view and whatever evidence he produces will be slanted in the direction which he wishes us to take. In the end we shall have to agree with him out of sheer weariness or oppose him on grounds which are already well known.[91]

Dowson was a man of strong views, difficult and temperamental in the eyes of some members of the Building Committee, but he enjoyed a good relationship with Southern, whom he called 'a gentle person with a spine of steel.'[92] Irritated by the college's indecisiveness, Kidd reported him as saying that:

---

[86] P. Dowson. 'St John's College, Sir Thomas White Building', *Arup Journal* xiv (Apr. 1979), p. 2.
[87] SJCA, Mun. lxxxi. 178(j).
[88] D. Chablo, 'University Architecture' , p. 84.
[89] SJCA, Mun. lxxxi. 170, 5 May 1971.
[90] SJCA, Mun. lxxxi. 179(c) 17 June 1971; Mun. lxxxi. (l); ADM I.A.13, p. 63.
[91] SJCA, Mun. lxxxi. 170, 18 Dec 1971.
[92] Conversation with author.

45 A drawing of the courtyard elevation of the east range of the Sir Thomas White Building, 1971. The slope in the site can be clearly seen

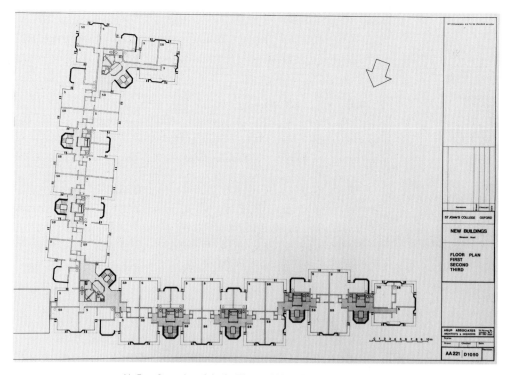

46 First-floor plan of the Sir Thomas White Building. North is at the bottom

he was used to dealing with Colleges, and understood the political stresses and strains involved, though he had to admit ... that he thought we were probably the most difficult he had ever experienced. He has never known a College before which was not prepared to delegate considerable authority to its New Building Committee; but he does understand that he is dealing with a College where the Governing Body is very reluctant to delegate any authority to anybody about anything.'[93]

Yet the Governing Body finally approved his design on 16 December, subject to a reduction in the height of the service towers so as to make them invisible from the North Quadrangle.[94]

A contract for £1,240,492 (excluding fees) was finally signed with the Cambridge firm of Johnson and Bailey in June 1972; by February 1983 this had gone up to £1,461,993, largely because of an estimated increase in the cost of the stone cladding for the service towers.[95] Construction began in the autumn of 1972, two years later than the starting date first envisaged in 1967, and early in 1973 a completion date was set for the beginning of Michaelmas term 1974.[96] The project was interrupted by delays, some of them blamed on the builders—who were apparently chosen because of their reputation for finishing projects on time—some on the architects, and others on extraneous factors for which both architect and builders disclaimed responsibility.[97] The company supplying the window frames went bankrupt in 1973 and the main contractors had to be bailed out for £40,000. And in 1975, when construction was largely finished, it was discovered that the sub-contractors had placed some of the metal reinforcement bars inside the concrete frame too close to the surface, so that the faulty sections had to be replaced.[98] Matters were not helped by the imposition of a three-day working week by Edward Heath's government following a miners' strike and interruption of power supplies in January 1974, and there were minor interruptions from the stoppages that plagued Britain throughout that troubled period.[99] But in the end the project, though delayed, was completed without a significant increase in cost over the original budget. The first rooms were ready for occupation in the autumn 1974, and the building was formally opened on 28 June 1975.

If the underlying metaphor of the Beehive is the cell, that of the Sir Thomas White Building is the skeleton. The building embodies three basic ideas: the use of a structural grid; the external expression of a reinforced concrete frame; and the separation of structure and services (Fig. 47). Like many of his contemporaries, Dowson laid great emphasis on the integrity of materials, especially concrete and

[93] SJCA, Mun. lxxxi. 179(c), 6 Dec 1971.
[94] SJCA, ADM I.A.13, pp. 93, 113.
[95] SJCA, Mun. lxxxi. 172; lxxxi. 178(m).
[96] SJCA, ADM I.A.13, p. 177.
[97] SJCA, Mun. lxxxi.179(d), 20 Jan 1973, etc; Mun. lxxxi. 178(m).
[98] SJCA, Mun. lxxxi. 172, 19 June 1975, etc. The defective parts were replaced, but an independent assessor judged that the frame as a whole was not defective.
[99] SJCA, Mun. lxxxi. 172, 18 Jan 1974, 8 Aug 1974, 13 Mar 1975.

47 The courtyard front of the Sir Thomas White Building, 1977 (© Arup Associates)

glass. And, like most architectural rationalists since the time of the French Enlightenment, he believed that there was a special virtue in making the construction of a building intelligible to the viewer, with the interior disposed according to a predetermined module and the different elements of the building clearly and logically demarcated from each other.[100] Of these elements the frame is the most important, not only in determining the construction and layout of the building, but also its visual character.

The idea of frame construction had been fundamental to modernist architecture ever since the pioneering days of the Chicago skyscrapers of the late nineteenth century. Equally powerful was the belief in the virtue of 'honestly' expressing the construction of a building on its exterior. If this could be achieved there would be no need for ornament, and the 'dilemma of style' that had plagued the nineteenth century could be solved. New building materials gave the architect the means with which to achieve this end. For Mies van der Rohe, writing in 1923, reinforced concrete buildings were by nature 'skeletal buildings . . . A construction of girders that carry the weight, and walls that carry no weight. That is to say, buildings consisting of skin and bones.'[101] Or, as one of Dowson's partners later wrote, the exposure of the frame 'produces a discipline . . . Showing the way a building is made has unquestionably considerable intellectual appeal but also creates within its own right a kind of grammar of decoration.'[102]

[100] Brawne, *Arup Associates,* p. 65.
[101] 'Working Theses', quoted in Conrads (ed), *Progams and Manifestoes,* p. 75.
[102] Brawne, *Arup Associates,* p. 47.

48 The Casa del Fascio, Como, Italy, by Giuseppe Terragni (1932–6). The clear external expression of the frame anticipates that of the Sir Thomas White Building (RIBA Library Photographic Collection)

Dowson was not the first architect to use the frame as the defining feature of a building's internal layout and external appearance. Antecedents can be found in some of the canonic buildings of modernist architecture, such as Terragni's Casa del Fascio in Como (1932–6) (Fig. 48) and the dry processes block at the Boots factory at Nottingham (1932), designed by the engineer Owen Williams. More recently, external frames had featured prominently in Skidmore, Owings, and Merrill's Banque Lambert in Brussels (1958–62) and Vigano's Istituto Marchiondi in Milan (1959).[103] Dowson made the external frame a personal trademark, first in his Vaughan/Fry Building for Somerville College on Little Clarendon Street, and later in his buildings for Corpus Christi College (Fig. 49) and Trinity Hall, Cambridge, in his Department of Metallurgy and Mining at the University of Birmingham (1964–6) and in the New Museums Building at Cambridge (1964–71).[104] On the wall of his office there was a picture of a balconied wooden house in Anatolia, which he admired because the balcony created an 'intermediate space' between the outer and inner worlds: a phenomenon also seen in the traditional Japanese architecture so admired by modernist architects of his generation. The frame in Dowson's Leckhampton Building for Corpus Christi College, Cambridge, was interpreted by one of his colleagues as an 'outer lace curtain', creating 'a three-dimensional layering of space and thus the appearance of depth

---

[103] See Banham, *New Brutalism*, pp. 43, 53, 127–8, 153–7; Chablo, 'University Architecture', p. 182.
[104] Chablo, 'University Architecture', pp. 116–17.

49 The George Thomson Building in the garden of Leckhampton House, built for Corpus Christi College, Cambridge, to Dowson's designs in 1962–4 (Cambridge 2000)

50 The Sir Thomas White Building from St Giles. Middleton Hall is on the left and the North Quadrangle to the right, with the President's drive—turned into a car park—between them (© Arup Associates)

without mass'.[105] A similar effect was intended in the Sir Thomas White Building (Fig. 50). In a letter to Southern, Dowson suggested that it would achieve an effect of 'security, seclusion, restfulness and generosity'[106] and he later wrote that '[we] aimed to exploit the richness and unity that can at once be derived from the diverse use of repetitive elements, and the various strands that can be woven within strict disciplines, which can help to identify the "part" within the "whole", and so help to create a sense of belonging'.[107]

[105] Brawne, *Arup Associates*, p. 47. See also Booth and Taylor, *Cambridge New Architecture*, pp. 146–8.
[106] SJCA, Mun. lxxxi.17(c), 1 Nov 1971.   [107] *Arup Journal* xiv (Apr 1979), p. 2.

51 One of the pre-cast elements of the Sir Thomas White Building being lifted into place (© Arup Associates)

The residential pavilions were not so much constructed as assembled, with the frames put together, like permanent scaffolding, from H- and half-H-shaped elements of pre-cast reinforced concrete (Fig. 51) made from a Ballidon aggregate from Derbyshire, similar to that employed in some of the firm's earlier work and chosen for its ability to weather well.[108] The concrete of the posts and beams was 'bush-hammered' to give it an almost sculptured appearance, and the sculptural effect was further enhanced by placing the uprights in pairs, with an uninterrupted vertical break between them; by splaying the right angles between the horizontal and vertical sections (Fig. 52); and by incorporating a notch at the junction of each pair of pre-cast sections. The glazing of the rooms is placed behind the frame, with sliding windows—of plain glass, not the tinted glass that Dowson originally wanted[109]—stretching from floor to ceiling.

Like Louis Kahn in his famous Richards Medical Laboratories in Philadelphia (1957–65) (Fig. 53)—a building much admired in the 1960s and 1970s for its sculptural power and its 'honest' expression of function—Dowson believed in the clear separation of 'served and 'serving' areas in a building. The Sir Thomas White Building was therefore broken up into discrete elements. The service (staircase) towers introduce a vertical note to balance the insistent horizontals of the frame and, with the pitched-roofed lead-clad 'pavilions' on the top floor, help satisfy

[108] Ibid., p. 4; conversation with author.
[109] SJCA, Mun. lxxxi. 172, 20 May 1972.

52 Concrete detailing on the
Sir Thomas White Building
(© Arup Associates)

the deep-rooted English love of broken skylines, avoiding the monotony that dogs many modernist buildings of the period (Figs. 54–5). The appearance of the towers was much enhanced by the college's decision to use stone: a decision supported by Dowson, though not originally by Southern, who had argued that it 'was associated with a certain timidity and even a clinging to old illusions'.[110] Both Portland and Clipsham stone were considered at first, but they were rejected in favour of a light-coloured limestone ashlar from the St Maximin quarries near Senlis in France. Similar in both colour and appearance to the Caen stone used in many medieval English buildings, St Maximin stone had been used in the restoration of Chichester Cathedral and of the Palais de Luxembourg in Paris, and it had the advantage of being both cheaper and more readily available than Clipsham, largely because of a more mechanized quarrying technique.[111]

The internal layout was conditioned by the need to squeeze a very large number of rooms into a limited space. The building is two rooms deep, with the bar and

[110] SJCA, Mun. lxxxi. 179 (c), 25 Nov 1971.
[111] SJCA, Mun. lxxxi. 172, 20 May 1972; *Arup Journal* xiv (Apr 1979), p. 4.

53 The Richards Medical Laboratories, Philadelphia, by Louis Kahn (1957–65). In this much-admired building the 'served' and 'serving' areas were clearly differentiated both internally and externally, as Dowson was to do in the Sir Thomas White Building (Corbis)

54 The southern end of the Sir Thomas White Building from the college garden (Chris Andrews)

55 The Sir Thomas White
Building at roof level
(© Arup Associates)

56 A view under the colonade
of the Sir Thomas White
Building (© Arup Associates)

57 One of the covered walkways in the Sir Thomas White Building (© Arup Associates)

Common Rooms placed on the ground floor, behind a 'cloister' running along the inner face (Figs. 56–7); the Middle Common Room occupied the rooms at the southern end of the east range. Dark and low-ceilinged, these rather cheerless spaces—one of them (the present Larkin Room) originally dubbed the 'departure lounge' by the undergraduates—lack the unpretentious comfort of the old Junior Common Room in the Front Quadrangle (Fig. 58). Upstairs the accommodation for 155 students, mostly undergraduates, is divided equally between bed-sitting rooms and two-roomed sets, with the sets facing south and west onto the courtyard and the bed-sitting rooms—usually allocated to first-year students—facing north and east (Fig. 59). The top floor consists of a series of penthouse-like flats for the Fellows, with terraces outside affording panoramic views over the gardens. A porter's lodge was created at the west end of the block flanking Museum Road. Access to all the rooms is through the towers, which contain staircases, toilets, showers, and shared self-catering kitchens (a novel feature of student life in the 1970s) as well as the bedrooms of the sets. The building has been understandably criticized for its cramped staircases and service areas, but this was probably a price that had to be paid if the rooms were not to become unacceptably small. And most students, faced with the choice between larger rooms and wider staircases, would probably opt for the former.

58 A drawing by Arup Associates of the interior of the bar in the Sir Thomas White Building

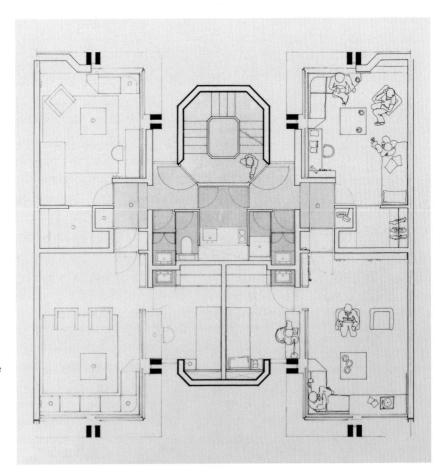

59 A plan showing the standard layout of rooms in the Sir Thomas White Building. The staircase is at the top, between two bed-sitting rooms. The lower rooms are sets, with the bedrooms placed between the two sitting rooms. The service areas are between the staircase and the bedrooms of the sets

60 A view from a room in the Sir Thomas White Building, looking south over the college garden to the hall of Balliol College (© Arup Associates)

The building was designed to be looked from, not only to be looked at; Dawson thought of the rooms as balconies, and Tim Sturgis, one of his partners, believed that the large windows would help overcome 'the sense of isolation which can occur in multi-storey buildings' (Fig. 60).[112] The rooms are indeed light and, especially by the standards of most university accommodation of the 1970s, they are spacious. Their layout and furnishing reflect Dowson's interest in shaping the domestic environment: an interest derived from the environmental determinism of the pioneering modernists of the 1930s, such as Wells Coates, the designer of the Lawn Road Flats in Hampstead, where the resident intellectuals could share communal facilities.[113] Southern had vainly protested that '[one] of the greatest faults that I have noticed in modern residential buildings is that the architect too often tries to impose his own vision down to the smallest details on the unhappy residents. I should like people to have large neutral spaces to make themselves at home in as they think best.'[114] But Dowson's views prevailed. He asserted in 1969 that:

[112] *Architectural Review* (Dec 1969), quoted in Chablo, 'University Architecture', p. 152.
[113] *Arup Journal* xiv (Apr 1979), p. 12.
[114] SJCA, Mun. lxxxi. 179(b), 22 Jul y 1971).

loose pieces of traditional furniture—in a multi-activity room of minimal area such as a study bedroom—practically never provide any real flexibility . . . the aim is to provide enough flexible built-in facilities and to provide smaller loose components in order to give the student a greater possibility for participating in creating his own environment.[115]

The rooms therefore contain built-in bookcases, cupboards, and window seats, designed by his colleagues and by the firm of Gordon Russell.[116] But the most notable internal features are the sliding wooden screens placed in front of the windows, and between the sitting rooms and bedrooms—or sleeping alcoves—in the two-roomed sets (Fig. 61). They ensure privacy from the gaze of the outside world, while at the same time imparting an attractive element of Japanese-style intricacy and domesticity.

The building was carefully integrated into its surroundings. A rubble-stone wall on the Museum Road side nestles behind the concrete frame at ground level, ensuring that the blankness so often found on the ground floors of large modernist buildings is avoided (Figs. 62–3). The site slopes slightly from west to east, and from north to south, making it possible for Dowson progressively, and almost imperceptibly, to reduce the height of each of the residential blocks so that the southern end of the east block, visible from the college garden, is six feet lower than the west end of the building. The building also gains from its landscaping. The gardens of the demolished Museum Road houses were levelled, and, by taking in the former presidential vegetable garden,[117] a courtyard was created and trans-formed over the years from a bare lawn into an attractive area of trees and shrubs enfolded by Dowson's skeletal blocks and towers (Fig. 64).

[115] SJCA, Mun. lxxxi. 170, 26 Nov 1969.
[116] SJCA, Mun. lxxxi. 172, 11 Feb 1974, etc. The cost was £283,500.
[117] SJCA, Mun. lxxxi. 172, 16 Nov 1975; 179(h), 30 Sept 1976.

62 The Sir Thomas White Building from Lamb and Flag Passage (Chris Andrews)

63 The south side of Museum Road, showing numbers 25–31 and the Sir Thomas White Building (Chris Andrews)

64 A recent photograph of the southern end of the Sir Thomas White Building, showing the mature planting (Chris Andrews)

Soon after the opening ceremony in the summer of 1975 Tim Sturgis told Southern: 'It has taken an amazing amount of time and thought to create this thing . . . Sometimes, for us in the trenches, it does seem a laborious process, worthwhile I'm sure if there is some achievement of cultural expression.' Yet, in a revealing comment, he added: 'Perhaps the College's ambitions were more practical.'[118] Southern thought that the building was 'a practical expression of the continuity of the College; and it links the present state of the College with its Founder in the most tangible, as well as symbolic, way'.[119] First conceived at a time when architectural modernism carried all before it, it takes its place alongside Ahrends, Burton and Koralek's impressive and adventurous buildings for Keble College at the junction of Blackhall Road and Museum Road (1973–7) as one of the last expressions of the modernist ethos in Oxford's collegiate architecture, at least until recent years. Public opinion had never wholeheartedly embraced modernist architecture; now, in the wake of a series of highly publicized architectural and urbanistic disasters, architects began to turn against it too. Pitched roofs and cosy vernacular detailing began once more to make an appearance, not least in the Squash Courts block, built to Dowson's designs immediately to the east of the Sir Thomas White Building (Fig. 65). Arup Associates introduced Frank Lloyd Wright-

[118] SJCA, Mun. lxxxi. 179(f), 7 July 1975.
[119] Speech at opening ceremony.

65 The exterior of Dowson's Squash Court before its partial transformation into the Middle Common Room. The garden wall is on the right.

inspired pitched roofs in their headquarters building for Lloyd's at Chatham and their Central Electricity Generating Board headquarters at Bedminster, near Bristol, both begun in 1973, and it was Dowson who carried out the renovation of the Snape Maltings in Suffolk as a venue for Aldeburgh Festival concerts: an exemplary fusion of the modernist ethos with the emerging spirit of architectural conservation.[120] In some respects therefore the Sir Thomas White Building expresses the spirit of an age that was already passing when it was completed.

The new building brought about permanent changes in both the physical and the social character of St John's. By 1977, 361 students were housed in college: twice the number before the Second World War.[121] Not only did most undergraduates now spend their first, and in some cases their second, years in the new accommodation; with the relocation of the Junior Common Room the college's centre of gravity shifted towards the north. Now that it was able to house all its undergraduates for the whole of their time in Oxford, St John's found that it had a competitive edge over most of its rivals in attracting able applicants. The number of first-class degrees leapt from 16 in 1979—when, crucially, women were first admitted—to 31 in 1984, and in five out of the six years from 1981 to 1986 St John's topped the Norrington Table of examination results.[122] So the new building can be said to have played an important part in raising the college's academic profile. Put up at a time of acute economic difficulty, soaring inflation, domestic and international tension, and growing disillusionment with the post-war social and political consensus, it is an expression of confidence which the experience of the last thirty years has shown to be fully justified.

[120] See Brawne, *Arup Associates*.
[121] *College Record* (1977).
[122] *College Record, passim*.

4 Upper and Nether Worlds: the Garden Quadrangle

St John's entered the last decade of the twentieth century in a buoyant state. During the 1980s it had usurped the place once occupied by its neighbour and rival Balliol as the college most consistently at the top of the Norrington Table of final examination results. The writer of the *College Record* for 1984 commented that the unprecedented number of 31 first-class degrees that year 'speaks volumes for the policies of recent years, for effective selection and (dare we say?) for competent tutorial guidance'; by 1994 the college was being described as one of 'Oxford's traditional academic powerhouses'.[1] By 1998 there were 68 Fellows and research Fellows, along with varying numbers of temporary college lecturers.[2] The size of the student body also grew to reach 532 by 1990 and 540 (including 164 postgraduates) in 1998. By the turn of the century there were three times as many resident members as there had been before the War.

None of this could have happened without financial resources. Until the 1970s much of the college's wealth had been tied up in land, both farms and the North Oxford estate of leasehold houses. Its modern prosperity derives from decisions made in the late 1960s and 1970s, during the bursarships of Harry Kidd and William Hayes, who succeeded him in 1977.[3] The most important of these decisions was to move out of land and house property and to invest the profits of the sales in higher-yielding urban property and equities. By 1990 property, including offices and shops, accounted for 55 per cent of the college's endowment, investments for the remaining 45 per cent.[4] As a result of the economic expansion that transformed the country under the Conservative administrations of the 1980s and 1990s, the value of both the property and the investment portfolio rose. It was this which enabled the college to contemplate building on a yet more ambitious scale at a time when, under the same administrations, the public funding of English universities was entering a period of crisis from which it has yet to emerge.[5]

The immediate occasion for building was a decision by Oxford University to vacate its Rural Economy Building, erected in 1906–8 on ground leased from St John's at the north-east corner of the garden, facing South Parks Road (Fig. 66). This quadrangular stone structure was designed by N. W. and G. A. Harrison,

---

[1] *College Record* (1994).
[2] *College Record* (1998).
[3] Hayes become President in 1987 after the retirement of Sir Richard Southern's successor Sir John Kendrew.
[4] Bursary Files, 'Finance', memo by Finance Bursar 29 Oct 1990.
[5] See R. Stevens, *University to Uni* (London 2004), *passim*.

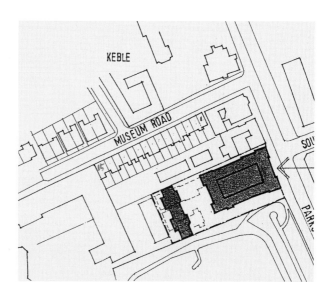

66 Plan of the Rural Economy site (shaded)

architects of the Rawlinson Building in the North Quadrangle, in an inoffensive version of the free style employed by their flashier contemporary, Thomas Graham Jackson (Fig. 67). It contained lecture rooms and laboratories and was extended in the 1930s. After the war, under the aegis of Geoffrey Blackman, Sibthorpian Professor of Rural Economy, important research was carried out there into weed control in order to raise crop yields, one of the fruits of which was the planting of yellow-flowered oilseed rape and blue linseed in fields all over Britain.[6] In 1985 the Rural Economy department was merged with the departments of Forestry and Botany to become the Department of Plant Sciences, and plans were set in motion to house all three in a new building to be funded, at least in part, by private sources, central government funding for such purposes having fallen victim to spending restrictions imposed by the government of Margaret Thatcher. The lease of the building was due to revert to St John's in 2012, but if St John's could be persuaded to pay the University a substantial sum for giving up the lease early, extra funding for the new building would accrue, and St John's would come into possession of a site within the periphery of the college on which it could build.[7] The Governing Body agreed to pay the University £350,000 at the beginning of 1988, and the college could now turn to consider what kind of building it wanted, and for what purpose.

In a sense the failure to build the whole of Philip Dowson's first scheme for expanding the college had left St John's with an unfinished architectural agenda. The decision to build the Sir Thomas White Building on a smaller site than the one originally earmarked meant that the 'public' parts of Dowson's original scheme had to be excised—with the exception of the student common rooms—in order

---

[6] SJCA, Mun. lxxxi. 230(a), 18 Oct 1991.
[7] SJCA, Mun. lxxxi. 230(a), 10 Dec 1987. The new Plant Sciences building went up behind Hubert Worhington's Department of Forestry in South Parks Road.

67 The east façade of the Rural Economy Building (Chris Andrews)

to fit in an increased number of student rooms. So the college still lacked the extra library accommodation, lecture room, and meeting room for the Governing Body which had been thought desirable in the 1960s. Nor had the Sir Thomas White Building totally solved the college's accommodation problems. All undergraduates could now be housed in college, but the ever-growing number of graduate students were given accommodation for only one year (or two if they came from outside Oxford University), leaving them to find rooms outside for the rest of their period of study. The rising price of property in Oxford made this more and more expensive, a rise caused in part by inelastic supply and in part by the growing number of students in other educational institutions such as Oxford Polytechnic (or Oxford Brookes University as it was soon to become).

It was the need for more postgraduate accommodation—first identified by Arthur Garrard in 1964—that prompted Anthony Boyce, a biologist who succeeded William Hayes as Bursar in 1987, to set in motion the process that led to the building of the Garden Quadrangle. One of his first acts as Bursar was to turn numbers 19–21 St John Street into twenty-five bed-sitting rooms for graduate students, a project carried out by the locally based Oxford Architects Partnership in 1987–8. And it was the Oxford Architects Partnership—a firm extensively employed in and around Oxford during the 1980s—which was approached in 1988 to prepare a feasibility study for the Rural Economy site. The study, submitted in April 1988, suggested a conventional layout of lecture and seminar rooms grouped around a quadrangle occupied by a dining room and auditorium, both of which could be used for conferences: an important source of revenue, though less so for St John's than for some colleges. Study-bedrooms would go on the upper floors, and more student rooms in a separate block to the west.[8] The existing façade to South Parks Road, which was listed Grade 2—the lowest listing category—would be preserved, and a version of the firm's rather timid house-style was suggested for the remaining elevations. The City of Oxford planners accepted this proposal in principle, and insisted that the South Parks Road frontage of Harrison's building be retained.

In comparison with the vicissitudes attending the Sir Thomas White Building, the Garden Quadrangle project proceeded smoothly and amicably. Howard Colvin, who had retired in 1987, warned William Hayes, now the President, that a clear brief, with no subsequent changes of mind, was 'always the basic requirement for a satisfactory architectural solution',[9] and his advice was followed. The task of framing the brief and searching for an architect was delegated to a Building Committee made up of six Fellows, none of whom had been involved in the Sir Thomas White Building; it began to meet in February 1989,[10] a month before the lease of the Rural Economy Building was surrendered by the University.[11] By now the Governing Body had decided to demolish everything except the façade, and to erect behind it 'high quality housing for junior members', mainly graduate students, together with an auditorium for lectures, plays, and musical perform-ances, a dining and reception room, extra library accommodation, and music practice rooms;[12] the cost was estimated at £3,338,450 plus value added tax. Consultations now took place with the undergraduates and graduate students, and revealed that the graduate students, far from wanting an enclave of their own, preferred to live alongside the undergraduates. The undergraduates, for their part, following social trends that were now well established in Oxford, set great store by the provision of self-catering kitchens, but held to long-established Oxford custom in preferring a staircase to a corridor layout. The outline proposals prepared in July 1989 took these concerns into account. The new building would contain fifty rooms for junior members, both undergraduate and postgraduate, together with six to eight rooms for Junior Research Fellows and academic visitors. There would be staircase access and shared kitchens. The auditorium would accommodate up to 250 people, and there would be space for up to 600 metres of library shelving.

The long, narrow site presented both problems and opportunities for an

---

[8] SJCA, Mun. lxxxi. 230(a), Apr 1988.

[9] SJCA, Mun. lxxxi. 230(a), 17 Jan 1989.

[10] SJCA, Mun. lxxxi. 230(a), 25 May 1988, 1 Feb 1989. The original members of the committee were the Bursar; Ross McKibbin (a historian); John Pitcher (English literature);Nicholas Purcell (ancient history); a scientist, Professor Llewelyn-Smith; and a mathematician, Paul Tod. Oliver Jacobs (engineering science) joined the committee at a later stage.

[11] A short-term lease was issued to allow the Plant Sciences department to remain in possession until 1991.

[12] SJCA, Mun. lxxxi. 230(a), 15 Feb, 8 Mar 1989

imaginative architect. Slightly below the level of the college garden, and sloping a little from east to west, most of it was taken up by the Rural Economy building which, behind its undemandingly agreeable east façade, consisted of a collection of undistinguished brick structures arranged around a courtyard, most of it filled in at a later date. There was a narrow passage to the north and a larger space inside the garden wall to the south, most of it used for car parking. To the west were assorted shed-like structures abutting onto the college Squash Courts, recently built to Philip Dowson's designs with student accommodation above, and beyond them was the east range of the Sir Thomas White Building. The main constraints on an architect, apart from the need to preserve Harrison's façade to South Parks Road, were the high rubble-stone wall to the south that imparted an essential sense of enclosure to the college garden; and the existence to the north of a row of stuccoed terraced houses on the south side of Museum Road, belonging to Lincoln College and separated from the St John's property by a narrow patch of ground housing Lincoln's own squash courts. These constraints played a large part in dictating the solution adopted by the architect who was eventually chosen.

The 1980s had seen the return to Britain of the 'Battle of the Styles' that had enlivened architectural debate in the mid-nineteenth century. Then Gothicists had confronted classicists; now the modernist architectural establishment, so recently in the ascendant, was attacked by a motley but vocal group of post-modernists, New Urbanists, neo-Georgians, conservationists, and assorted eclectics, led—at least in the mind of the popular press—by the Prince of Wales, whose notorious speech in 1984 attacking Ahrends, Burton and Koralek's 'carbuncle' design for the National Gallery articulated many people's concern at the direction British architecture had taken in the 1960s and 1970s. The reaction against modernist architecture can be taken back to the 1970s, when pitched roofs and cosy brick surfaces with neo-vernacular detailing—anathema to hard-core modernists— began to creep back into private and eventually, into public buildings, as at the much-publicized Hillingdon Civic Centre in west London (1976–8) and even in the universities.[13] The election of Margaret Thatcher's Conservative government in 1979 was followed by an era of consumer prosperity and rampant economic individualism in which pit-heads were replaced by shopping malls, factories by estates of bijou residences. In such an environment it is not surprising that architectural style should itself become a matter of consumer choice.

The change that took place in British architecture between the mid-1970s, when the Sir Thomas White Building was completed, and the late 1980s is exemplified by the designs sent in for consideration in October and November 1989. Five firms were approached, but one, that of Robert Adam, a classical architect who later went on to design the Sackler Library next to the Ashmolean Museum, declined to compete.[14] The four competing firms were noticeably

---

[13] See S. Lyall, *The State of British Architecture* (London 1980); Chablo, 'University Architecture', pp. 208–13.
[14] SJCA, Mun. lxxxi. 230(a), 5 May 1989. The Oxford Architects Partnership was not asked to compete.

smaller and—with one exception—less well-known than those that had entered the last architectural competition held by St John's in 1967. Julian Bicknell and Partners was a London-based firm of only four partners, two of whom were architects and two designers. Bicknell studied architecture at Cambridge and later worked with Hugh Casson, Edward Cullinan, and Arup Associates before entering independent practice in 1983, by which time he had already built up a reputation for designing new buildings and alterations to old buildings in environmentally sensitive places: an important aspect of architectural practice in an increasingly conservation-minded age. He was responsible for the renovation of the early-nineteenth-century Old Gaol in Abingdon as an arts and leisure centre in 1972, and in 1984 he designed the Gothic case for the new organ in Magdalen College chapel. Meanwhile he had built up a successful practice as a designer of new country houses, including the neo-Palladian 'Villa Rotonda' at Henbury (Cheshire) for Sebastian de Ferranti (1983), and he was also responsible for redecorating the former Saloon or garden hall at Castle Howard (Yorkshire) in 1980 out of the proceeds of the television adaptation of Evelyn Waugh's *Brideshead Revisited*. Robert Maguire and Ian Salisbury (Maguire & Co.) were the successors of the long-established firm of Maguire and Murray, designers in 1958–60 of the pioneering modernist church of St Paul, Bow Common in East London. Maguire later became head of the School of Architecture at Oxford Polytechnic and, with Murray, designed a number of collegiate buildings in Oxford, including the clumsy Cumberbatch Building at Trinity (1964–7) and the visually much more satisfying Geoffrey Arthur Building for Pembroke on the south bank of the River Thames to the west of Folly Bridge (completed in 1989). The third firm, the Cambridge-based Saunders Boston, grew out of a practice started in the 1930s by C. H. James, architect of the City Hall at Norwich—a good example of the Scandinavian-influenced 'stripped classicism' favoured at that time—and was responsible for a number of competent if unspectacular buildings in East Anglia, including the Fisher Building next to Powell and Moya's Cripps Building at St John's College, Cambridge, completed in 1987.

The firm to have achieved widest recognition in recent years was that of Mac-Cormac Jamieson and Prichard. Richard MacCormac had, like Bicknell, gone to the Cambridge University School of Architecture during the 1960s, when, under the direction of Leslie Martin and Colin St John Wilson—architect of the British Library—it had been one of the leading nurseries of architectural talent in England. Having worked with Powell and Moya and the modernist firm of Lyons, Israel and Ellis, he set up partnership with Peter Jamieson in 1972 and during the 1970s and early 1980s worked on a number of the most innovative public, shared-ownership, and private housing schemes in the new city of Milton Keynes.[15] When public

[15] e.g. the Chapter House development of flats at Coffee Hall (1975–7); houses at France Furlong (1977–80) and Cottisford Crescent (1978–81) at Great Linford; Tranlands Close at Heelands (begun 1979); Nursery Gardens at Bradwell (1982).

68 The Sainsbury Building at Worcester College, Oxford, by Richard MacCormac 1980–3) (Chris Andrews)

housing dried up after 1979, under the Thatcher government, the firm switched its focus to university work, designing a number of buildings which responded to the growing demand by clients and the wider public for a style of architecture that respected the historic environment and created a welcoming, unintimidating sense of place.[16] The first of these schemes was the Sainsbury Building at Worcester College, Oxford (1980–3) (Fig. 68). Coming only five years after the completion of the Sir Thomas White Building, this engaging lakeside complex of brick-clad, pitched-roofed student rooms introduced a new and friendlier architectural idiom into an Oxford that had been dominated for the previous two decades by the language of modernism, sometimes in its most brutal[17] or eccentric[18] forms. This was followed by a new range of rooms at Fitzwilliam College, Cambridge, by Blue Boar Court at Trinity College, Cambridge, and by the Bowra Building at Wadham College, Oxford, elements from all of which can be seen in the design that MacCormac prepared for St John's.[19]

[16] Marcus Binney in *The Times Saturday Review* (29 Jan 1991).
[17] e.g. Dowson's Nuclear Physics complex in Banbury Road (1967–70), and the Zoology and Psychology Building in South Parks Road (Leslie Martin, 1966–71).
[18] e.g the Florey Building for The Queen's College (James Stirling, 1968–71).
[19] A list of of the firm's work can be found on its website, www.mjparchitects.co.uk. Work in other universities included the Arts Faculty at the University of Bristol (1979–88) and student housing and the Information Technology Building at Queen Mary College, University of London (1986–9).

69 Design by Julian Bicknell for the Rural Economy site, 1989. The buildings face south to the garden wall

70 Design by Maguire and Co. for the Rural Economy site, showing the frontage to Parks Road

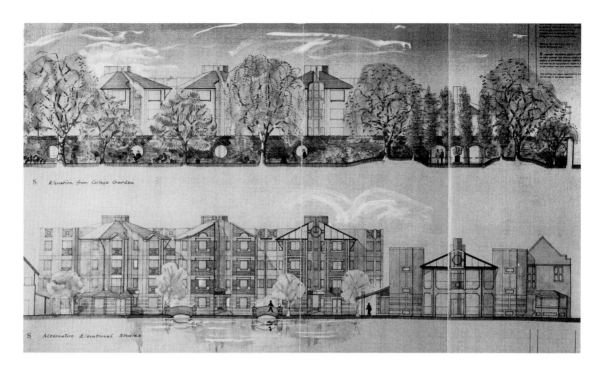

71 Design by Saunders Boston for the Rural Economy site

Two of the competitors adopted courtyard plans for the site. Julian Bicknell proposed an open-ended courtyard facing south to the garden wall, with the auditorium squeezed between it and the east range of the Rural Economy building, which would contain the music practice rooms.[20] The library shelving would go on the ground floor of the new courtyard building behind a cloister, with the students' rooms on three floors above. Bicknell's proposed architectural treatment was somewhat bland, with pitched roofs and rendered brick elevations, '[echoing] without mimicking the pattern of the rest of the College and Oxford as a whole'(Fig. 69). Maguire's solution was more adventurous.[21] He too proposed an open south-facing courtyard of pitched roofed buildings with assertively projecting windows (also a feature of his building at Trinity College) on the western part of the site, enclosing a water garden with a walkway created at first-floor level along the inner face of the garden wall. The centre of the east range of the Rural Economy building would be demolished—something that would have led to difficulties with the City planners and Conservation Officer—and replaced with a wide archway leading into a forecourt which would give access to the octagonal auditorium, placed next to the east range of the residential building (Fig. 70); the book storage would go under the courtyard. Saunders Boston proposed a very different solution.[22] They too would have placed the auditorium behind the east range of the Rural Economy building, but instead of a courtyard to the west they

[20] 'The Development of the Rural Economy Site', Julian Bicknell and Associates, Oct 1989.
[21] 'The Agricultural Science Site: Feasibility Study for St John's College', Maguire and Co., Oct 1989.
[22] 'St John's College, Rural Economy Site', Saunders Boston, Nov 1989.

suggested building three linked pavilions of masonry construction, with pre-cast concrete floors, arranged in a semicircle around an artificial lake, each of them four storeys high with a pitched roof (Fig. 71). In this way the firm hoped to avoid the 'claustrophobic feel' of the Sir Thomas White Building and to impart a sense of 'real elegance'.

72 Sir Richard MacCormac (MacCormac Jamieson Prichard)

Richard MacCormac (Fig. 72), the author of his partnership's design, admired the Sir Thomas White building, and in certain respects he echoed it in his own scheme, while adopting a radically different layout and a much more varied architectural vocabulary.[23] Since the Sainsbury Building at Worcester College he had developed a new and more monumental style for collegiate architecture, first seen in an unexecuted scheme of 1986 for new buildings for the same college flanking Hythe Bridge Street.[24] This site, like the one at St John's, was bounded by a high wall which had to be retained, so MacCormac devised a plan whereby the student accommodation would be placed in concrete framed towers on top of a terrace or 'raised place' with a lecture or conference room underneath. The concept of grouping accommodation on a raised site was perhaps influenced by Alvar Aalto's famous town hall of 1949–52 at Säynätsalo (Finland). But Mac-Cormac departed from modernist practice by introducing decorative ideas derived from other sources, including the architecture of Elizabethan England and the English Baroque of Sir John Vanbrugh and of Nicholas Hawksmoor, who had been involved in the original design of Worcester College in the 1720s. In his external treatment of the concrete frame MacCormac also proposed a system of 'vertebrate architecture', emphasizing the trabeated nature of the construction by isolating the upright and horizontal members. The phrase 'vertebrate architecture' had been used by Howell, Killick, Partridge and Amis in connection with their Senior Combination Room at Downing College, Cambridge (1966–70).[25] And MacCormac believed that it was also applicable to the Sir Thomas White building, which he compared to 'cabinet work, with the glazing contained in the masonry structure'.[26]

Such eclectic mingling of modernist with historicist ideas would not have pleased the previous generation of architects. But it was becoming increasingly acceptable in an age of post-modernist rejection of absolute architectural standards, in which architecture was being interpreted not only as structure but also as an organized system of signs conveying meaning. Disenchanted with the alleged sterility of the modernist vision of a mechanistic future, architects were rediscovering the allure of the past and casting off the Miesian belief that 'less is more' in favour of a renewed love of ornament and variety for its own sake. Such ideas had been provocatively aired by the American architect Robert Venturi in his *Complexity and Contradiction in Architecture* (1966) and had been zealously—if not always very

[23] 'St John's College, Development of Rural Economy Site', Richard MacCormac, Oct 1989.
[24] *Architectural Review* (May 1989), pp. 68–75.
[25] *RIBA Journal* 77 (1970), p. 106.
[26] *Architectural Review*, p. 71.

clearly—publicized in England by the architectural writer Charles Jencks, notably in *The Language of Post-Modern Architecture* (1977). MacCormac was more lucid in his inaugural address as President of the Royal Institute of British Architects in 1991, pointing out that 'to regain public confidence, modern architecture needs to relate to the past, evoking tradition without compromising authenticity', pleading for an end to futile 'style wars', and drawing attention to the creative interplay between past and present seen in the work of such architects as Frank Lloyd Wright and Carlo Scarpa.[27] It is debatable to what extent the term 'post-modern' can be usefully applied to the work of Richard MacCormac, but post-modernism certainly helped create an intellectual environment in which his style of architecture could become acceptable.

MacCormac's second design for Worcester College failed to please the college's main benefactor, Lord Sainsbury, and in 1988 he was dropped as architect in favour of Maguire and Co., whose Linbury Building now occupies the site. But he had already had the opportunity to experiment with 'vertebrate architecture' in the New Court at Fitzwilliam College, Cambridge, completed in 1986, where the highly ingenious interiors call to mind, *inter alia*, Charles Rennie Mackintosh, Frank Lloyd Wright, and the architecture of Japan. He followed this with the Blue Boar Court at Trinity College, Cambridge (1988–90), where he succeeded in squeezing a lecture room and accommodation for fifty students into an exceptionally confined site hemmed in by listed buildings and overshadowed by the monumental and formidably impressive Wolfson Building by the Architects' Co-Partnership (1972). Here the brick-clad residential buildings were placed around a courtyard on a platform at first-floor level with shops—including the local branch of Sainsbury's—and service delivery areas below. At Wadham College, Oxford (1988–92) (Fig. 73), on a narrow and confined site not unlike the Rural Economy site at St John's, MacCormac also raised the main residential areas onto a terrace and grouped them into towers reminiscent of those in the rejected Worcester scheme, and of Hardwick Hall, Derbyshire (1590–7), placing the common rooms at ground level (Fig. 74). Here he introduced elements of 'vertebrate architecture' in the concrete posts and beams that contrast with the expanses of yellow brick walling. But oversized classical or Mannerist elements also intrude into the first-floor 'internal street' along which much of the accommodation is placed, and such features were soon to reappear at St John's.

MacCormac's plan for St John's was classical in inspiration, with the main elements symmetrically placed and the layout axial. As in his rejected scheme for Worcester College, and in Blue Boar Court at Trinity College, Cambridge, and the Bowra Building at Wadham, he proposed to raise the residential accommodation onto a terrace and to place the 'public' rooms—the auditorium and, in the original

---

[27] www.mjparchitects.co.uk/essay/pursuit/html. For MacCormac's philosophy of architecture, see also 'Modern Architecture: Collecting the Baggage of Tradition', *Architecture Today* (Sept 2003), www.mjparchitects.co.uk/essay/pursuit/html.

73 The Bowra Building at
Wadham College by Richard
MacCormac (1988–92)
(Chris Andrews)

74 Hardwick Hall, Derbyshire
(1590–7), one of the greatest
'prodigy houses' of the
Elizabethan era (English
Heritage, National
Monuments Record)

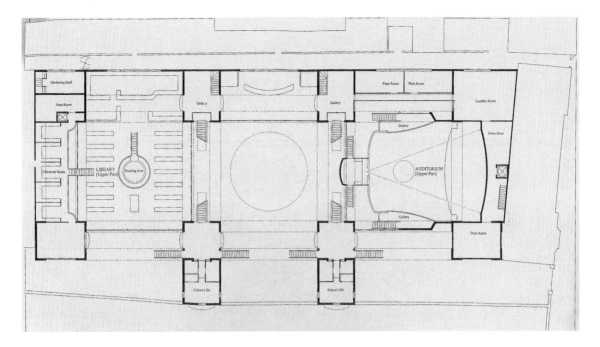

75 Richard MacCormac's first design for the Garden Quadrangle (1989), ground-floor plan. A library occupies the position of the present auditorium and the auditorium is on the site of the present dining/reception room

plan, the library—at ground level, separated from each other by a courtyard lit from above (Fig. 75). Thus the problem of the garden wall, and that of separating the two distinct requirements, for private and for public rooms, would be settled in a lucid and easily comprehensible fashion. The contrast between the shadowy, mysterious ground level and the light, open upper terrace was one that fascinated him, and in his report he carefully inserted an erudite reference from Rabelais: 'The greatest treasures and most wonderful things lie hidden underground—and not without reason.'[28]

From the garden only the upper levels of the building would be visible (Fig. 76), grouped in towers as at Wadham to create a skyline comparable to that of Sir John Vanbrugh's buildings (Fig. 77). The study-bedrooms, like those of the Sir Thomas White Building, would be arranged around staircases, and in the first plans each room would have its own bathroom; there would also be self-catering kitchens. The rooms would look out onto a raised garden on the terrace, from which there would be views out to the trees and lawns of the college garden. Since it would normally be approached from the side—either from the Sir Thomas White Building or from South Parks Road—the ground level would be revealed sequentially, in a manner 'analogous to that of the classical English country house, normally approached from the side, but formally confronting its park',[29] as at Vanbrugh's Blenheim Palace and Castle Howard. The ground level was to be an 'underworld', offering 'a kind of sanctuary discovered through an opening and addressed on either side by cavernous spaces brightly lit within'; a perspective

[28] *Gargantua and Pantagruel* 5:48.
[29] Bursary drawings file, Oct 1989.

76 Revised design for the Garden Quadrangle, cross-section (1990), showing the auditorium and dining room in their present positions

77 Seaton Delaval, Northumberland, by Sir John Vanbrugh (1718–29) (English Heritage, National Monuments Record)

drawing showed the central courtyard overrun with lush foliage, with a group of students playing lutes and other Renaissance instruments in the 'belvedere' or gazebo over the entrance (Fig. 78). Scenes of a grotto at Würzburg in Germany, of Alexander Pope in his grotto at Twickenham, and of one of the top-lit banking halls at Sir John Soane's Bank of England were inserted into the text, and at a later stage MacCormac referred to the top-lit rooms in the Golden House of Nero in Rome. No wonder the design appealed to a Building Committee whose members included both a historian and a classicist.

Of the designs submitted, MacCormac's, whose three options ranged between £9,500,000 and £11,000,000, turned out to be by far the most expensive.[30] But it was he who won over the Governing Body, partly through his verbal presentation, and partly through the intrinsic qualities of imagination and inventiveness shown

[30] Bursary files 'Initial Papers'. Julian Bicknell turned out to be the cheapest, at £6¼ million. See SJCA, Mun lxxxi.230(a), 24 Nov 1989.

78 First design for the Garden Quadrangle, perspective view from the garden entrance

in his designs, and in a vote on 29 November 1989 he received the support of twenty-one of the fellows, to Bicknell's twelve, Saunders Boston's eleven, and Maguire's seven.[31] He therefore received the commission, subject to a cost limit of £7,000,000 at 1989 prices: a sum later adjusted to £10,000,000 (including fees) to take account of inflation, which was once again rising rapidly.[32] The funding was to come from capitalizing income from both property and investments—further sales in North Oxford, sales of retail property, and bonds—over a ten-year period, with the aim of restoring the level of the endowment in the long term.[33] But first the brief had to be modified in order to match it to the budget. A 'cost plan' had been drawn up for the Bowra Building for Wadham College, and a quantity surveyor from the firm of Northcroft, Neighbour and Nicholson, who

[31] SJCA, Mun lxxxi.230(a), 29 Nov 1989; information from Ross McKibbin.
[32] SJCA, Mun lxxxi.230(a), 8 Jan., 14 Feb 1990.
[33] SJCA, Mun lxxxi.230(a), 7 Feb 1990, Mun lxxxi(b), 31 Oct 1990; Bursary files, 'Finance', 19 Oct, 29 Oct 1990. There was also a bequest from a former Rhodes Scholar, Frederick Russell Gamble: *College Record* (1988).

had worked on the Wadham project, was appointed in January 1990 to draw up a similar plan for St John's.[34] He advised that substantial savings could be made by detaching the new building from the existing Rural Economy building, thus ensuring that it would not be liable to the value added tax levied on alterations to existing structures.[35] MacCormac had already suggested making further savings by down-grading the proposed library—which was originally planned to go on the western side of the building—into a simple bookstack, and these modifications were incorporated in MacCormac's revised design, submitted in March 1990.[36]

Under MacCormac's new scheme an open space was to be opened up between the new building and the east range of the Rural Economy building, the rest of which was to be demolished. The library reading room would be omitted and the dining/reception room placed on the western side of the new building, under the terrace, with the auditorium in a corresponding position to the east. Despite these changes, the scheme still turned out to be 14 per cent over budget, and MacCormac was asked to make further savings by reducing the size of the auditorium to 200 seats and the dining room to 125.[37] These changes were made, and in April he submitted another design, which was further modified in August by reversing the positions of the auditorium and dining room, thus allowing the former to take advantage of the slight slope at the western end of the site. This design provided the basis for the building that we see today.[38]

Though the scale of MacCormac's scheme was reduced from that first revealed to the college in October 1989, the main principles remained the same. A series of 'residential pavilions' were to be grouped around the raised quadrangle (Fig. 79), each one containing up to ten rooms, with four rooms on each of the two lower floors, arranged around a central lobby after the fashion of Thomas Rickman's New Court at St John's College, Cambridge (1825–31). As in MacCormac's earlier building at Fitzwilliam College, the kitchens would be placed on the half-landings to encourage sociability: students, he told Marcus Binney in an interview in 1991, 'often get depressed. I think it is a result of isolation. We placed all the kitchens at the top of staircases so that anyone going to make a cup of coffee is sure to meet whoever is coming and going.' (Fig. 80).[39] The forty-four rooms would no longer have the *en suite* bathrooms originally planned, and in the upper rooms the beds would be placed in mezzanine galleries; the four sets for Junior Research Fellows would be placed closest to the garden and would 'engage' the garden wall, and there would be six more undergraduate rooms in the remodelled remnants of the Rural Economy building. The 'public' rooms, each 10.8 by 10.8 metres, would go under the terrace, as originally planned, and the library book store in the basement

---

34 Bursary files, 'MJP', 7 Aug 1989; SJCA, Mun lxxxi.230(a), 17 Jan 1990.
35 Bursary files, 'Letters to Contractors', 24 Nov 1989, 26 Jan 1990, 15 Mar. 1990.
36 SJCA, Mun lxxxi.230(a), 5 Mar. 1990.
37 SJCA, Mun lxxxi.230(a), 16 Mar. 1990.
38 'St John's College, Development of Rural Economy Site', Richard MacCormac, Apr. 1990, with appendix 19 June 1990; Bursary drawings file, SJC 102, 112.
39 *The Times Saturday Review* (29 June 1991).

79 Model of the Garden
Quadrangle

of the Rural Economy Building. Space was also found on the ground floor, next to the dining/reception room, for a gallery in which to preserve and display the college's superb collection of pre-Reformation ecclesiastical vestments. The open space next to the Rural Economy Building was to be occupied by an 'attractive, identifiable little building' housing music practice rooms (Fig. 81).

Concrete was to be the main constructional material, with the 'public' rooms on the ground floor covered by vaults supported on free-standing columns. Given the nature of the design and the limitations of the budget, the choice of concrete was inevitable. The Romans had used a form of concrete for their domes and vaults, but in modern times the technology of concrete for arches and vaults did not evolve until the early twentieth century.[40] Shell-concrete vaults had been an essential component of the Architects' Co-Partnership's Brynmawr factory,[41] and concrete offered MacCormac the opportunity to create satisfying and memorable internal spaces faster and more economically than would be possible with masonry construction. In the words of the structural consultant, Sam Price of Price and Myers: 'Some people might ask why we don't use steel instead of concrete, but that is complete nonsense. They simply aren't alternatives—you use a different material and you get a different building. In St John's everything is integral to the design: the frame is the structure is the finish.'[42] The vaults would be protected by the earth or paved surfaces of the raised courtyard above: a principle which, MacCormac said, 'offers a stable, durable and highly insulated covering to the public accommodation'.[43] The residential 'pavilions', by contrast,

[40] R. Mainstone, *Developments in Structural Form* (Harmondsworth 1975), pp. 130, 225–7; V. Perry, *Built for a Better Future* (Oxford 1994), pp. 37–8.
[41] See Fig. 14, p. 26.
[42] *Building* (11 March 1994), p. 38.
[43] Bursary papers, 'St John's College, Development of Rural Economy Site'.

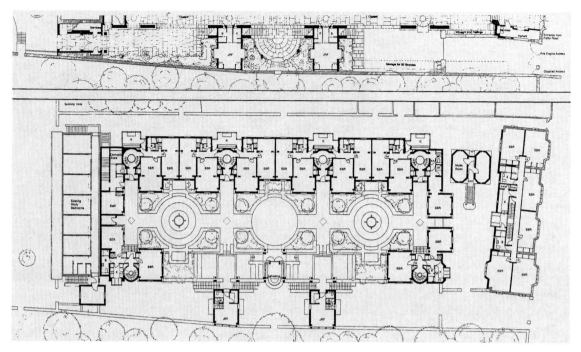

80 The Garden Quadrangle, plan of terrace and student accommodation

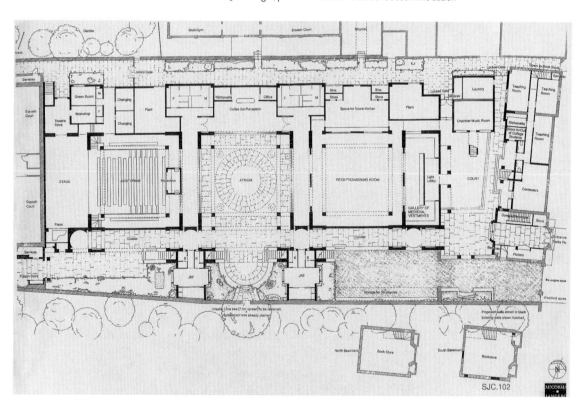

81 The Garden Quadrangle, ground-floor plan

were to be of load-bearing construction, with *in situ* concrete floors, pre-cast staircases and external walls combining brickwork with pre-cast concrete, and zinc- or lead-covered roofs. Following some minor alterations to the design during the summer of 1990, including a reduction in the size of the 'belvedere' and a redesign of the west façade of the Rural Economy building, planning permission was given in early 1991.[44] The plant scientists vacated the old building in the summer of that year, and the firm of Try Construction from Uxbridge, west London, won the contract for the new building in August 1991.[45] By this time MacCormac had become President of the Royal Institute of British Architects—ensuring wide publicity for the new building[46]—and the management of the project was handed over to one of his associates, Jeremy Estop.

As in most structurally sophisticated buildings of modern times, the role of the structural engineer was crucial. Philip Dowson drew on the engineering expertise of his partners in Arup Associates in designing the Sir Thomas White Building; MacCormac chose the firm of Price and Myers. Sam Price was involved in the crucial decision—taken after building had begun—to use pre-cast rather than *in situ* concrete for the main structural components supporting the 175-millimetre thick *in situ* domes and the terrace. This meant that the lower parts of the building had to be assembled from prefabricated units, made out of a creamy white Ballidon aggregate—also used in the Sir Thomas White Building—mixed with white Portland cement (Fig. 82). These units were expertly made by the Ely-based firm of Histon Concrete Products[47] and assembled on site by Try Construction, using timber centring, with extra reinforcement and *in situ* concrete (by the firm of Whelan and Grant) to stitch them together and provide extra solidity for the podium above: a process of considerable technical difficulty.[48]

The switch from *in situ* to pre-cast concrete increased the cost, and early in 1992 Try Construction requested an accelerated payment of £30,000; by February 1992 the contingency fund had been nearly used up.[49] Replying to remonstrations from the Finance Bursar, MacCormac insisted that the complexity of the design had 'produced more unforeseen problems in the resolution of details than traditional forms of construction'.[50] But there were also aesthetic gains to be made from the much greater variety of surface texture possible in pre-cast concrete:[51] an opinion from which anyone looking closely at the building today would find it difficult to dissent. Savings were made by using cheaper plaster finishes to the domes of the 'public' rooms and by reducing the size of the 'gatehouse' through which the building is entered at its western end, and in July

[44] SJCA Mun lxxxi(b), 5 Dec 1990.
[45] SJCA Mun lxxxi(b), 27 Aug 1990; Bursary papers, 'Tenders', 29 Aug 1991.
[46] See *Architects' Journal* 14 Nov 1990, pp. 14–17.
[47] The pre-cast staircases were made by Sindall Concrete Products.
[48] *Building* (11 Mar 1994), p. 38.
[49] SJCA Mun lxxxi(b), 12 Feb, 4 Nov 1992.
[50] Bursary files, 'Finance', 27 Aug, 25 Sept 1992.
[51] Bursary files, letters to contractors.

82 The Garden Quadrangle under construction, engraving by John Howard, commissioned by the College in 1992

1992 a revised cost of £6,945,265 was agreed.[52] The less technically complex upper levels followed swiftly after the completion of the ground floor, and the first twenty-five rooms were completed in time for Michaelmas term 1994; the building was finished by the end of that year. The final bill turned out to be £8,520,000 (or £10,140,000 if architects' fees and value added tax on the alterations to the Rural Economy building are included), plus £460,000 for furniture and fittings.[53] The name Garden Quadrangle was suggested by one of the Fellows, Ross McKibbin, after earlier suggestions to call it the Walton Manor building, in recognition of the contribution to the cost made by selling property on the Walton Manor estate in North Oxford, or the 'Southern Quadrangle'—after Sir Richard Southern—had been mooted but rejected.[54]

Soon after construction started in the autumn of 1991, old members of the college were invited to contribute to a fund for embellishing the new building with appropriate works of decorative art.[55] As a first step towards identifying the artists, the college approached Vivien Lovell, head of the Public Arts Commissions

[52] SJCA Mun lxxxi(b), 29 July 1992; Bursary files, 'Finance', 26 Nov 1992.
[53] Bursary files, 'Finance', 5 Jan 1994.
[54] One of the Fellows thought that it should be named 'Dunownin', in recognition of the college's sale of most of its landed assets: SJCA Mun lxxxi(b), 5 Mar 1993.
[55] SJCA Mun lxxxi(b), 28 Oct 1991.

Agency and former Visual Arts Officer of the London Borough of Tower Hamlets, within whose boundaries MacCormac's Spitalfields office was situated. Seven projects were identified: etched glass screens; paving panels; a garden gateway; sculpture on the axis of the gateway; chandeliers or glass reflectors in the 'public' rooms; railings in the open area between the new building and the remnants of the Rural Economy Building; and a fabric screen over the auditorium stage.[56] Soon afterwards Denis Moriarty, a BBC producer and old member of the college, was appointed to launch an appeal for £780,000, and in May 1992 a glossy brochure was sent to old members with a letter from the President, urging them to contribute to a scheme that would 'provide a unique opportunity for the College to be seen to take lead in Oxford in its commitment to architecture and the arts'.[57]

The artists selected for consideration were Wendy Ramshaw and the iron-worker James Horrobin (for decorative screens and railings, including a gateway into the garden); the glass artists Alexander Beleschenko, Jane McDonald, and Elizabeth Ogilvie (for glazed screens separating the auditorium and dining room from the central couryard or atrium); Richard Devereux, Brian Catling, and Simon Lewty (for 'narrative art works' on surfaces and walls); Anthony Gormley, Peter Randall-Page, and Vincent Woropay (for sculpture); Alexander Beleschenko and Wendy Ramshaw—again—for chandeliers in the two main 'public' rooms. The project was to start with works that were integral to the structure—the glass screens and the ironwork—and, in a brief for the artists and craftsmen, MacCormac drew attention to the contrast between the 'underworld' of the public areas and the 'overworld' of the raised courtyard: there should be 'a sense of discovery about these [public] areas . . . Seen through the glazed screens from the central space, the two large rooms will appear dark and mysterious, top-lit through cupolas and hollow key stones.'[58] Eventually two were selected: Alexander Beleschenko, designer of windows at the Hampshire County Council offices in Winchester and the International Convention Centre in Birmingham, and Wendy Ramshaw, best-known for her jewellery. Beleschenko would design the glass screens at a cost of £100,000, and Ramshaw the garden gate—her largest commission to date—for £25,000. Old members of St John's, unlike those of less fortunate colleges, were not accustomed to being asked for money, and the response to the appeal was somewhat disappointing. But work on the screens and the gate went ahead, the total cost coming to £154,495, £20,982 of which went in fees to the Public Arts Commissions Agency.[59]

The Garden Quadrangle reveals itself piecemeal and episodically in a manner 'designed to sustain a sense of the secretive and unexpected'.[60] It is usually

[56] Bursary files, 'Art and Architecture', 11 Nov 1991, 6 Feb 1992.
[57] 'Art and Architecture: the St John's College Project', May 1992.
[58] Bursary files, 'Art and Architecture', 8 June 1992, etc.
[59] Bursary files, 'Art and Architecture', 13 Jan 1994.
[60] C. Slessor, 'Oxford Ordonnance', Architectural Review 193 (Oct 1994), p. 43; Bursary papers, brochure produced by MacCormac, Jamieson and Prichard after the building's completion.

83 The southern approach to the Garden Quadrangle. The block in front contains flats for Junior Research Fellows (MacCormac Jamieson Prichard)

approached from the west, through the courtyard of the Sir Thomas White Building and past the former squash courts erected by Arup Associates and subsequently turned into the Middle Common Room.[61] An opening or 'gatehouse' leads past the garden wall into what MacCormac has called a crypto-porticus (Fig. 83)—a term signifying a subterranean passage in ancient Roman architecture—giving access to the auditorium and the dining/reception room, each of them 10.8 metres square and each with a shallow dome of 8.6 metres radius.[62] They are placed on either side of the central atrium—used in its ancient Roman sense of a courtyard open to the sky—into which daylight penetrates through an open hoop or *oculus* (Fig. 84), producing an effect of sharply contrasted light and shadow that were prompted in MacCormac's mind by the engravings of ancient Roman buildings produced by the eighteenth-century Italian architect and artist Giovanni Battista Piranesi (Fig. 85). The classical mood is sustained by the ingenious Latin 'chronogram'—an inscription in which the letters that are also Roman numerals add up to the date 1993—composed by Nicholas Purcell, a member of the Building Committee, and carved on a stone panel inside the remodelled east range of the Rural Economy Building: OECONOMIAE RVRALIS ATRIA COLLEGIO DIVI IOHANNIS BAPTISTAE ATTRIBVTA OPEQVE EIUS RESTRVCTA HOSPES INIS.[63]

[61] See pp. 129–131.
[62] *Building* (11 March 1994), p. 38; *Concrete* (Sept./Oct. 1994), p. 8.
[63] Visitor, you are entering the Rural Economy Buildings which were returned to St John's College and rebuilt at the college's expense.

84 The central courtyard
of the Garden Quadrangle,
watercolour by Ilana
Richardson from the
Oxford Almanack, 1995
(© Oxford University Press)

85 Ruins of the Statue Gallery
at Hadrian's Villa, Tivoli, by
Piranesi, c.1770, from *Veduti di
Roma* (Ashmolean Museum)

86 The dining and meeting room in the Garden Quadrangle (MacCormac Jamieson Prichard)

87 The Breakfast Room at 13 Lincoln's Inn Fields, London (1812–13) (By courtesy of the Trustees of Sir John Soane's Museum)

Constructionally, the most important elements are the shallow segmental arches resting on massive piers that define each of the three main spaces and support the terrace above.[64] In Roman or Renaissance architecture these would have been of brick or stone, but here, despite first appearances, they are entirely of pre-cast concrete assembled on site, with carefully contrived variations of surface treatment designed to express the weight of the building and the different purposes of each structural element. In High Renaissance and Mannerist architecture structural meaning is often conveyed through the texture of masonry, notably by the use of rustication at the lower levels to emphasize heaviness and solidity and smoother ashlar for the more important parts of the building above. In the Garden Quadrangle MacCormac used heavily pointed rustication to emphasize the weight of the supports and a smoother needle-gunned or grit-blasted treatment for the arches and the pendentives, each of them weighing 8.2 tonnes, that carry the *oculus* of the atrium and the domes of the auditorium and the dining/reception room.[65] The idea of making concrete look like stone would have offended the modernist architects of the previous generation, just as it would have enraged John Ruskin and other critics who have found it hard to divorce architectural judgement from questions of moral integrity. But concrete is an adaptable material which can be made to produce whatever effect the architect wishes. There were many precedents in Renaissance architecture, not least in the work of Palladio, for the use of stucco to imitate stone, and in the Garden Quadrangle MacCormac adapted that approach to the materials and technology available in the late twentieth century.

If Piranesi is the presiding spirit in the approaches to the auditorium and dining room, it is Sir John Soane who springs to mind inside (Fig. 86). Soane—who, like Piranesi, was captivated by the buildings of Roman antiquity—was a conscious exponent of what he called the 'poetry of architecture', often achieved by the conscious manipulation of light and shadow. He was fascinated by domes and top-lighting, and his idiosyncratic buildings contain several examples of rooms roofed with shallow domes resting on segmental arches and pierced at the top to admit light from above: an effect that can still be seen in the Breakfast Room in his own house (now Sir John Soane's Museum) at 13 Lincoln's Inn Fields, London (Fig. 87). MacCormac's dining room and auditorium are larger versions of the Breakfast Room in Soane's house, though on a much larger scale and with much shallower domes.[66] As at Lincoln's Inn Fields, the domes define the character of each room, but they are handled in a manner which introduces a note of spatial complexity, by resting on pendentives that are supported not at the corners of the rooms but by clusters of free-standing pre-cast columns standing just inside each corner, rather

---

[64] This can be clearly seen in an axonometric drawing of Oct 1990 in the bursary files, SJC 127.
[65] *Building* (11 Mar 1994), p. 36.
[66] The domes also echo the Soanean dome designed by Howard Colvin for the Sadler Room in the Senior Common Room: see Fig. 109, p. 127.

88 The auditorium in the Garden Quadrangle, looking from the stage to the entrance (MacCormac Jamieson Prichard)

89 The courtyard seen through the glass screen by Alexander Beleschenko to the auditorium (Chris Andrews)

90 The display room for the 'Laudian Vestments' (MacCormac Jamieson Prichard)

as in the 'internal cruciform' arrangements of some of Sir Christopher Wren's City churches (themselves reminiscent of Byzantine architecture). This allows a walkway to be created around the edge of each room; in the auditorium this becomes a raised gallery, due to the fact that the ground level is sunk (Fig. 88). Since the walls are not load-bearing the openings to the atrium could be completely glazed, and Beleschenko's screens, each with 30,000 tiny pieces of glass inserted in abstract patterns, ensure that the light is subtly modulated; the effect was intended to suggest 'running water and the crystalline structure of rocks' (Fig. 89).[67] To the west of the auditorium is the stage, and in a corresponding position to the east of the dining room is the gallery for the medieval vestments, entered from the courtyard adjoining the Rural Economy Building (Fig. 90). The space along the north side of the building is occupied by changing and other ancillary rooms for the auditorium and by kitchens attached to the dining room—allowing it to become a self-contained building—with a reception area in between.

[67] Bursary papers, 'Art and Architecture', file on Beleschenko; article on the new artwork by Ruth Pavey from an unknown publication.

The atrium is the focal point of the building: an outdoor room which mediates between the lower and upper levels and enables the visitor to get his or her bearings (Fig. 91). Here the effect is deliberately romantic. Plants hang over the edges of the *oculus*, as in Piranesi's engravings, and chains descend to the ground from circular openings in the pendentives (Fig. 92). They are designed to carry rainwater down from the raised terrace above—an idea also seen in the Architects' Co-Partnership's Dunelm House at the University of Durham[68]—but by their thinness they also point a contrast to the massiveness of the surrounding structures and add to the atmosphere of the 'enigmatic Piranesian underworld'.[69] The archway nearest the garden wall is surmounted by a glazed 'belvedere' reminiscent of eighteenth-century follies or garden pavilions (Fig. 93), and beyond it is Wendy Ramshaw's garden gateway, made of fabricated steel at Rowland Quinnell's Rowhurst Forge in Surrey. The gate consists of two parts, the lower one made up of upright bars supporting an off-centre circular motif—a feature of some

[68] I owe this point to Sir Howard Colvin.
[69] *Architectural Review* 193 (Oct 1994), p. 43.

92 One of the arches supporting the terrace of the Garden Quadrangle (MacCormac Jamieson Prichard)

of Ramshaw's jewellery—in which a lens is placed (Fig. 94). Ramshaw recalled MacCormac telling her that 'he wanted something poetic, unlike other ironwork. So my drawings were unlike any other gates I have seen'; for her the lens showed the observer 'what you would have seen anyway, but detached, and swimming in a rather brilliant, magnified roundness'—a symbol of the 'curious and enquiring mind'.[70] Beyond the gate is the natural arcadia of the garden, from which the towers of the upper level of the Garden Quadrangle—a 'miniature San Gimignano'[71]—can be seen above the trees (Fig. 95).

MacCormac's architecture has always been marked by a love of complexity, almost for its own sake, and by a fascination with surfaces: characteristics also found in Italian Mannerist architecture and in the buildings of Vanbrugh and Hawksmoor. The surface of the upper courtyard is treated as a roof garden, with raised concrete borders enclosing beds of earth for shrubs, punctuated by two glazed lanterns—almost like minature circular classical temples—lighting the

[70] G. Darley, 'Pulling Together', *Royal Academy Magazine*, (Summer 1994), pp. 38–9; Bursary papers, 'Art and Architecture', file on Wendy Ramshaw gate and article by Ruth Pavey. The hinges on the gate were placed on the wrong side at the forge, meaning that it is seen the opposite way from what was intended by the artist.
[71] *Concrete*, (Sept/Oct 1994), p. 8.

93 The gazebo, or belvedere, and the garden gateway from the courtyard (Chris Andrews)

94 The garden gateway by Wendy Ramshaw (Chris Andrews)

rooms below (Fig. 96). In the residential buildings surrounding the courtyard, as in the earlier New Court at Fitzwilliam College, pre-cast concrete elements are introduced in juxtaposition with plain brickwork to produce an effect that calls to mind Japanese timber architecture. The result is to emphasize the trabeated nature of the construction—in contrast to the omnipresent arches of the ground level—and also to point a visual link to the Sir Thomas White Building, where towers also punctuate the skyline (Fig. 97).[72] These textural effects are carefully modulated, with plain brickwork at the lower level, horizontal slabs of concrete at floor level and surfaces of what MacCormac has called 'an astonishing smoothness' in the concrete posts and beams at the top: an effect achieved, according to the manager of Histon Concrete Products, as 'the result of a wet process using several types of grit and a combination of rotary and orbital polishing machines, finished off by washing down the units, applying Italian marble polish and then buffing it off'.[73] The

[72] Catherine Slessor, the writer of the article in *Architectural Review* 193 (Oct 1994), pp. 43–9, saw analogies with the strongly trabeated architecture of Karl Friedrich Schinkel and 'Greek' Thompson.
[73] *Building* (11 Mar 1994), p. 36.

95 The upper level of the Garden Quadrangle as seen from the garden (MacCormac Jamieson Prichard)

96 The terrace of the Garden Quadrangle. The lantern to the dining/reception room is in the foreground (MacCormac Jamieson Prichard)

97 The central towers of the Garden Quadrangle from the courtyard (MacCormac Jamieson Prichard)

tiny gargoyle-like projections for rainwater may be inspired by Stirling and Gowan's famous housing development at Ham Common in south-west London (1968): one of the best-known buildings from the early years of the 'New Brutalism'. The architectural effect becomes more complex at the higher levels, notably in the surrounds of the top-floor windows and the abstract arrangements of free-standing posts and beams above the projecting cornices at roof level. They echo the pinnacles and crenellations of medieval towers or the 'eminencys' (as Hawksmoor called them) at Blenheim Palace. Thus the romantic classicism of the lower regions gives way to romantic medievalism above.

The study-bedrooms are of varying sizes and shapes, and each has a bed alcove separated from the main study area (Fig. 98); in the rooms at the tops of the towers the beds are placed in sleeping galleries (Fig. 99).[74] The rooms are reached by circular staircases clad in finely tooled concrete (Fig. 100)—anticipating the similar treatment in the firm's Jubilee Line station at Southwark on the London Underground—and they look out onto the courtyard, thus avoiding the isolation and alienation of some student residences; the kitchens are placed on the outer faces of the building. The two flats for Junior Research Fellows occupy lower

[74] Bursary papers, drawings file.

98 One of the student rooms in the Garden Quadrangle (MacCormac Jamieson Prichard)

99 One of the top-floor rooms in the Garden Quadrangle, showing the sleeping gallery (MacCormac Jamieson Prichard)

100 A staircase in the Garden Quadrangle (MacCormac Jamieson Prichard)

self-contained pavilions overlooking the garden, each with its own staircase and kitchen.

In the Music Room block, between the main quadrangle and the remodelled Rural Economy Building on the eastern part of the site, MacCormac experimented with a different, and starker, architectural treatment (Fig. 101). The ground level is heavily rusticated, but the upper rooms are hexagonal—perhaps in allusion to the Beehive building—and the façades take the form of canted bays in plain brick surmounted by a more heavily emphasized version of the free-standing post-and-beam roofline employed in the towers of the quadrangle. Here perhaps we see the germ of the design used by MacCormac in his Jowett Building for Balliol College (completed in 1996; second phase under construction at the time of writing). Adjacent to the music block is the remodelled west façade of the Rural Economy building—a successful piece of pastiche—given over to teaching rooms and computer rooms, with more study-bedrooms above.

The Garden Quadrangle was an expensive building, but the college bore the cost with equanimity, and pride in MacCormac's achievement soon outweighed any residual grumbles about expenditure. More than any building put up by the

101 The Music Rooms and the remodelled west elevation of the former Rural Economy Building (MacCormac Jamieson Prichard)

college since the Canterbury Quadrangle, it caught the public imagination, winning numerous awards and being voted Best Building of 1994 by the *Independent* newspaper.[75] In his inaugural address as President of the Royal Institute of British Architects in 1991 MacCormac quoted the Italian architect Giancarlo de Carlo, who was responsible for the conservation and extension of the Renaissance town of Urbino:

To design in a historic place one should first of all read its layers of architectural strata and try to understand the significance of each layer before superimposing a new one. This doesn't mean to indulge in imitation, as that would be a mean-spirited approach, saying nothing about the present and spreading confusion over the past. What is called for is the

[75]   See Jonathan Glancey's article in *The Independent* (26 Jan 1994).

invention of new architectural images to be authentic and at the same time reciprocal with images already existing.[76]

The Garden Quadrangle exemplifies this philosophy. As the *Architectural Review* commented, MacCormac had set out to 'civilise its users rather than institution-alise them',[77] and he achieved this aim with such success that it became the most popular, as well as the most aesthetically pleasing, of the buildings put up by St John's since the Second World War.

---

[76] The text of the speech can be found on the firm's website, www.mjparchitects.co.uk/essay/pursuit/html

[77] *Architectural Review* 193 (Oct. 1994), p. 49.

5 Into the Twenty-First Century: the Queen Elizabeth House Site

An 'architectural promenade'—to borrow a phrase from Le Corbusier—through the post-Second World War buildings of St John's presents the history of modern architecture in England in microcosm, from the cautious conservatism of the immediate post-war years in the Dolphin Quadrangle to the self-confident modernist experimentation of the Beehive; and from the assured and uncompromising modernism of the Sir Thomas White Building to the allusive *fin-de-siècle* subtlety of the Garden Quadrangle (Fig. 102). These buildings also embody the recent history of the college itself. Now, as this book goes to press, plans are being prepared for yet another expansion that could have as profound an effect on its social and architectural character as the construction of the Sir Thomas White Building in the 1970s. Medieval Oxford was largely contained within its walls, but from an early date houses had been built along the main streets leading into the city. St Bernard's College, whose buildings St John's took over in 1555, was itself part of this early example of 'ribbon development', and by 1675, when Ralph Loggan published his map of Oxford, St Giles, the broad, tree-lined thoroughfare along which Oxford is approached from the north, was lined with houses on both sides. The houses on the eastern side, together with their substantial gardens, had all come into the college's hands by the end of the twentieth century, and it is at the northern end of this row of houses that the planned expansion is to take place.

The incorporation of the St Giles houses into the college began in 1905 when, not long after the completion of the street frontage of the North Quadrangle, and shortly before the construction of the Rawlinson Building,[1] a modest two-gabled rubble-stone house was converted by N. W. Harrison into sets of rooms reached from the north quadrangle, with an office for the estate collector on the ground floor.[2] Middleton Hall, to the north of the President's drive, was likewise taken over, and turned into undergraduate rooms in 1936.[3] Beyond lie four properties taken over by the college, renovated and turned into student rooms in 2000–1; they include the Lamb and Flag, a stuccoed timber-framed structure whose ground floor is still used as a public house, and two stone-fronted houses of the late eighteenth or early nineteenth century (numbers 14–15 St Giles) (Fig. 103). The handsome house of 1702 now known as St Giles House, immediately to the

[1] See p. 3.
[2] *Oxford Chronicle* (13 Oct 1905), p. 9.
[3] G. Tyack, *St John's College: A Short History and Guide* (Oxford 2000), p. 57.

102 A bird's-eye view of the college in the 1990s from the south-west, by Paul Draper

north, has been in the hands of the college since 1964, and attached to its northern end is a more modest three-storeyed eighteenth- and nineteeth-century house (numbers 17–19) which may, under plans currently (2004) being considered, eventually be turned into accommodation for the President, thus freeing the current President's Lodgings on the eastern side of the Front Quadrangle for other uses (Fig. 104).[4]

The Queen Elizabeth House site lies to the north of these houses (Fig. 105). It is made up of a heterogeneous collection of buildings and their gardens, most of which have since 1961 formed part of Queen Elizabeth House, a centre for the study of the developing countries founded in 1954 and merged in 1985 with the Institutes of Commonwealth Studies and Agricultural Economics.[5] On the southern part of the site is number 20 St Giles, an attractive early nineteeth-century bow-windowed villa used for many years as a tutor's house. Black Hall, further north, is a stone-fronted house dating from the first part of the seventeenth

[4] 'Accommodation Stategy: Initial Report, St John's College, Oxford', Duncombe Parker Architects, 2003. The Accommodation Strategy also envisages an eastward extension of the Bursary and the building of a new Junior Common Room on the southern side of the Sir Thomas White quadrangle.
[5] C. Hibbert (ed.), *The Encyclopedia of Oxford* (London, 1988), p. 345.

103 The eastern side of St Giles, showing from left to right, Numbers 14–15, the Lamb and Flag, and Middleton Hall (Chris Andrews)

104 St Giles House (right), 17–19 St Giles (centre) and 20 St Giles (left) (Chris Andrews)

century with a three-storied gabled wing (Fig. 106); beyond it, past the plain 1961 entrance to Queen Elizabeth House itself, is a rubble-stone former barn. A pair of stuccoed, gabled early seventeenth-century houses belonging to the college lie on the northern extremity of the college's property, adjoining the University's Mathematical Institute, but are not part of the site. Under the current proposals the houses on the St Giles frontage, which are all listed, are to be preserved; the main Queen Elizabeth House buildings, however, which run east to west along the northern boundary of the spacious garden of the former Black Hall, are destined to disappear after the lease terminates and the property comes into the college's hands in October 2005.[6] They were put up in 1961, to the designs of R. E. Enthoven, and consist of a brick block with an extension to the east, in a bland and

---

[6] 'Queen Elizabeth House Site, St John's College, Oxford, Architectural Brief', 2004.

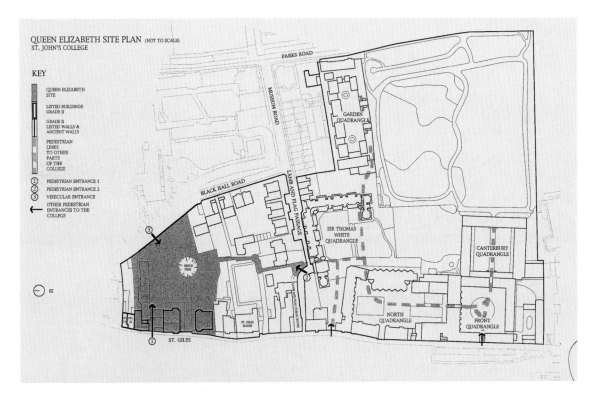

QUEEN ELIZABETH SITE PLAN (NOT TO SCALE)
ST. JOHN'S COLLEGE

KEY

QUEEN ELIZABETH
SITE

LISTED BUILDINGS
GRADE II

GRADE II
LISTED WALLS &
ANCIENT WALLS

PEDESTRIAN
LINKS
TO OTHER
PARTS
OF THE
COLLEGE

① PEDESTRIAN ENTRANCE 1
② PEDESTRIAN ENTRANCE 2
③ VEHICULAR ENTRANCE
← OTHER PEDESTRIAN
ENTRANCES TO THE
COLLEGE

PARKS ROAD

MUSEUM ROAD

GARDEN
QUADRANGLE

BLACK HALL ROAD

LAMB AND FLAG PASSAGE

SIR THOMAS
WHITE
QUADRANGLE

CANTERBURY
QUADRANGLE

BEECH
TREE

NORTH
QUADRANGLE

FRONT
QUADRANGLE

ST. GILES

105 A plan of the college in 2004, showing the Queen Elizabeth House site (shaded) on the left

inoffensive style of architecture that recalls some of the Scandinavian-influenced public housing schemes of the early 1950s.[7]

On the site of the Queen Elizabeth House buildings the college proposes to put up accommodation for between 80 and 100 students, both undergraduates and graduates, on either the staircase or corridor pattern, with *en suite* showers and WCs, and some communal rooms; there will also be a new library for law, and for science and mathematics. The Barn is to be turned into a building for the visual arts, with a gallery, studio, and dark-room, and Black Hall will be given over to tutorial rooms for Fellows and lecturers, and possibly one or more seminar rooms; the use of 20 St Giles remains to be decided. A new north–south pedestrian route will link the Queen Elizabeth House site to the main part of the college, running behind the garden of St Giles House and passing underneath the Lamb and Flag Passage before emerging into the Sir Thomas White quadrangle. When realized, these plans will enable not only all undergraduates but also all graduate students to be housed in college: an essential part of any future strategy for enhancing the character of St John's as a residential community of scholars. They will also bring to fulfilment plans first conceived by Arthur Garrard in 1964 for expanding the college to the north of Museum Road,[8] but without the loss of the Victorian houses in Museum Road and Blackhall Road which are now valued as an important part of Oxford's varied urban fabric.

[7] N. Pevsner and J. Sherwood, *The Buildings of England: Oxfordshire* (Harmondsworth, 1974), p. 270.
[8] See p. 47.

106 The older buildings on the Queen Elizabeth House site from the garden. 20 St Giles is on the left and Black Hall in the centre (Chris Andrews)

Eight firms of architects were invited in the spring of 2004 to submit preliminary designs to the college, with the intention of choosing four to go forward to a limited competition later in the year. At the time of writing no selection had been made. But, given the college's resources, and its record as a patron of good modern architecture, it is reasonable to hope that St John's will soon acquire a set of buildings of a quality comparable with those it has erected over the past fifty years, of which this book is intended to be both a record and a celebration.

Appendix I   **The Senior Common Room**

According to Anthony Wood, common rooms were first established in Oxford in the second half of the seventeenth century 'to the end that the Fellows might meet together (chiefly in the evening after refection) partly about business, but mostly for society's sake, which before was at each chamber by turns'.[1] In most colleges the common room—or Senior Common Room, as it became when junior members began to have their own common rooms—was created within the existing buildings of a college. But at St John's a new free-standing building was erected for the purpose in 1673–6, to the designs of the local mason Bartholomew Peisley the elder.[2] It was placed to the north of the Chapel, in what was to become the North Quadrangle, and its south-eastern corner adjoined the Baylie Chapel, built as a mortuary chapel for Richard Baylie (d. 1667), who had been reinstated as President of the college after the restoration of Charles II.

Peisley's common-room block was a modest stone building, one room deep, with a frontage of four windows at first-floor level above a basement and dormer windows lighting the rooms in the attic. On the first floor there was, and is, a single large room, handsomely panelled in oak and beautified by a splendid plaster ceiling put up by the local plasterer Thomas Roberts in 1742. In, or soon after, 1826 the building was extended north to the designs of Daniel Robertson, architect of the Oxford University Press buildings in Walton Street.[3] This extension contained a second, inner, room for the Fellows—later renamed the Middle Room—with a ceiling decorated by the firm of Frederick Crace and a frieze of classical texts, and a new entrance; externally it matched the plain style of the earlier building except on the roofline, which was flatter in pitch, following the fashion of the time. Then in 1900 another extension was made to the north, housing a Smoking Room which was attractively remodelled internally with oak panelling by Edward Maufe in 1936 (Fig. 107). This brought the long, narrow building up to the President's stables. Behind it were the kitchens of the President's Lodgings, dating from the nineteenth century and linked to the Lodgings themselves by a passage alongside the east end of the Chapel.

With the number of Fellows growing after the war, the existing rooms in the Senior Common Room block, impressive though they were, came to be seen as increasingly unsuitable not only for their needs but also for those of the growing numbers of peripheral academics on whom the college relied to carry on its

---

[1] Quoted in G. Tyack, *Oxford: an Architectural Guide*, p. 131.
[2] Colvin, *Dictionary*, p. 746; *VCH Oxon* iii, p. 262. Peisley's son, another Bartholomew, was probably the builder of St Giles House: see pp.117–8.
[3] Colvin, *Dictionary*, p. 823.

107 The Senior Common Room from the North Quadrangle. The original building of 1673–6 is to the right.

teaching. As the Bursar, Arthur Garrard, told the University Registrar in 1952: 'Occasions arise when Fellows are unable to come into Common Room after dinner and guests are a problem, and we only give very restricted Common Room rights to Lecturers and Demonstrators who are not Fellows but attached to the College.'[4] Plans had already been conceived by Maufe in the 1930s and drawn up by him in 1944 for relocating the President's kitchens to the ground floor of the Lodgings and replacing the existing kitchens with guest rooms, an enlarged Common Room, and a new Muniment Room to take the college's records, formerly housed in the fifteenth-century gate tower.[5] These plans were put in abeyance while the Dolphin Quadrangle was being planned and built.[6] but the project was revived in 1951, when Maufe submitted a design for doubling the width of the building, with a Muniment Room on the ground floor, a room for lunches and Governing Body meetings above it, guest rooms in the attic, and a neo-Georgian façade to the President's garden, featuring French windows opening onto a balcony at first-floor level; at the same time the steeply pitched attic storey

4   SJCA, Mun. lxxxi. 50, 24 June 1952.
5   SJCA, Mun. lxxxi. 45(1), 3 June 1943, 3 Oct. 1944; ADM. I.A.11, p. 232.
6   See pp. 10–17.

108 Booth and Lederboer's 1953–5 extension to the Senior Common Room, from the President's garden. The east end of the Chapel is to the left (Architects' Co-Partnership)

of the 1673–6 building on the North Quadrangle side would be continued north over the 1826 and 1900 extensions.[7]

Maufe resigned as architect rather than accept modifications to his plans suggested by the Bursar, notably to the height of the dormer windows facing the North Quadrangle and to the French windows, which the President, Austin Lane Poole, believed would impair the privacy of his garden. Maufe recommended that in his place the college should approach David Booth, a local architect who was in partnership with Judith Lederboer, well-known as a designer of public housing schemes. Booth sent in his drawings in 1952, but the work was not carried out until 1953–5, after the building licence system was removed, at a cost originally estimated at £26,500.[8] His building was radically different from the one proposed by Maufe. Constructed of concrete, faced with stone, with steel reinforcements to floors and roof, there was a blank flat-roofed façade of the utmost plainness to the President's garden, enlivened only by a set of windows lighting the new lunch and meeting room (Fig. 108). It was praised in qualified tones in the *Architectural Review* as an improvement on the messy arrangement of service buildings previously on the site,[9] but it was not a building to raise the spirits or quicken the imagination, and few tears were shed when it vanished in 2003 to make way for a

[7] SJCA, Mun. lxxxi. 50, 18 June 1951.
[8] SJCA, Mun. lxxxi. 50, 26 Oct 1951, 9 Jan, 24 June 1952; Mun. lxxxi. 168(ii); ADM I.A.11, p. 342. The firm went on to design the Waynflete Building for Magdalen College, on the far side of Magdalen Bridge, in 1960–1.
[9] 'Putting New with Old', *Architectural Review* 122 (Nov 1957), pp. 344–5.

new building by MacCormac Jamieson and Pritchard, due to be completed in 2004. From an aesthetic point of view the most positive result of the scheme was the remodelling of the roof facing the North Quadrangle.

During the 1960s the future of the building became entangled in the complicated story of the genesis of the Sir Thomas White Building. For a time it looked as if a new 'chapter house' for Governing Body meetings would be included in Philip Dowson's plans for the Museum Road site, thus removing some of the pressure on the existing building.[10] By now the number of Fellows had grown, and the prospect of further growth, not only of the fellowship but also in the number of research fellows and college lecturers, made enlargement seem essential, not only for a meeting room but also to relieve the pressure on the Smoking Room, an informal reception room designed for a fellowship only half the size which, by 1979, with between forty and fifty people lunching each day, had become 'intolerably overcrowded'.[11] The 'chapter house' idea was dropped early in 1970, by which time Dowson had prepared plans for extending the Senior Common Room by Building further east into the President's garden and creating a lunch and meeting room that could seat seventy-eight people; a revised version of his plans was submitted in June 1971.[12] But with work about to start on the Sir Thomas White Building (it began on 1972), anxiety about the cost, and about what some saw as Dowson's intransigent approach to architectural questions, caused the Governing Body to set his plans aside in May 1973.[13]

Meanwhile Howard Colvin, who had recently designed a house for himself in Plantation Road, was encouraged to offer his own solution to the problem of the Senior Common Room. On 14 March 1973 he told Richard Southern, the President, that 'Dowson's skeletal architecture will look fine on its own site, [but that he] would not personally welcome its intrusion into the older part of the College . . . Although it is a little embarrassing to supplant Dowson, I am very firmly of opinion that architects are there to serve their clients' wishes.'[14] He envisaged a two-storeyed structure in place of Booth's single-storey room, with a spacious sitting room over an enlarged lunch and meeting room, and Walter Price of the Oxford Architects' Partnership was engaged to estimate the cost. This, at £180,000, was judged too expensive,[15] and in 1975 Colvin prepared a less ambitious scheme for a new room in the north-east corner, in the L-shaped gap between Maufe's Smoking Room and Booth's lunch and meeting room. The awkward shape was resolved by subordinating the two arms to a dominant space covered by a shallow plaster spherical dome inspired by the work of Sir John

[10] See p. 55.
[11] SJCA, Mun. lxxxi. 139, 5 June 1979.
[12] SJCA, ADM I.A.12, pp. 383–4; ADM I.A.13, pp. 20, 42–3; Mun. lxxxi.170, 5 Feb 1971; Mun. lxxxi. 112; Mun. lxxxi. 140.
[13] SJCA, ADM I.A.13, p. 187.
[14] SJCA, Mun. lxxxi. 140, 14 Mar 1973.
[15] SJCA, ADM I.A.13, p. 214.

109 The interior of the Sadler Room in the Senior Common Room, designed by Howard Colvin and Walter Price and built in 1980–1

Soane;[16] a doorway in the west arm led to the Smoking Room, another in the south arm to the lunch room, thus improving circulation. The Governing Body finally made up its mind to go ahead with this scheme in 1979; detailed drawings were worked up by Colvin and Price, and the work was carried out in 1980–1 at a cost of £79,000 (Fig. 109).[17] Thus Howard Colvin's name was added to the tally of inventive amateur architects—George Clark, Henry Aldrich, Edward Holdsworth —who had enriched Oxford with their buildings.

At the time of writing (2004) the Senior Common Room is once more being enlarged, this time by the firm of MacCormac, Jamieson and Pritchard, who were responsible for the Garden Quadrangle. As so often in the recent architectural history of St John's, this is the realization, in a different architectural language, of an earlier abandoned project, that for an eastward expansion of the building prepared by Philip Dowson in 1971. The brief, prepared in 1999, mentioned the need for a larger lunch room, improved kitchens, and a better use of the ground and attic floors. Under the new plans, the Muniment Room has been removed to a temporary home in the basement of St Giles House and a new kitchen created at

[16] SJCA, Mun. lxxxi. 140, 22 May 1975, etc; Mun. lxxxi. 130.
[17] SJCA, Mun. lxxxi. 139; Mun. lxxxi. 110–11.

110 Richard MacCormac's proposal for the extension of the Senior Common Room, 2002

ground level, with a sitting room in the extension to the east; upstairs the lunch room is extended to accommodate thirty-six more people, and there is another sitting room and a roof terrace on the top floor.[18] Lifts are inserted, and there is plentiful provision for disabled access. The dining room rests on a cantilevered concrete slab, and the new east façade, or 'envelope', replacing Booth's rather unsatisfactory frontage to the President's garden, is a lightweight transparent structure of glass with a louvred timber screen within a steel and oak frame at first-floor level (Fig. 110). Described by the firm as 'more a garden pavilion than a rooted extension, allowing the natural surroundings of the garden to to reach into the building, rather than the building encroaching upon it',[19] the Common Room extension, like other recent projects in Oxford, such as the impressive Rother-mere American Institute (by Kohn, Pedersen and Fox), is a reminder that modern-ist architecture, when handled with sensitivity, can enhance, rather than detract from, a historic setting.

[18] 'St John's College Dining Room: detailed design proposal', MacCormac, Jamieson and Pritchard, September 2002.
[19] www.mjparchitects.co.uk/flash.html.

The Middle Common Room

The first Middle Common Room for graduate students in Oxford was established by Lincoln College in 1958.[1] At St John's a Middle Common Room was created in 1961 in one of the college-owned houses in Museum Road (Mansel House)[2] and this sufficed until the addition of the Sir Thomas White Building, when Mansel House was demolished and a new common room created on the ground floor of the new building. This was never a very satisfactory arrangement, partly because of the intrinsic disadvantages of the dark, noisy, low-ceilinged rooms, partly because some of the crucial facilities, notably the bar, were shared with the Junior Common Room. This became a problem as the number of graduate students grew during the 1980s and 1990s, an increasing number of them from overseas and many of them unwilling to share their social space with what they regarded as callow undergraduates with whom they had little in common.

A little to the east of the Sir Thomas White Building were the college's Squash Courts, erected to Dowson's designs at the same time as the main building but in a very different architectural style, with rubble-stone walls and a pitched roof: an example perhaps of a change in Arup Associates' house style that first became discernible in about 1973, and was later taken up by Richard MacCormac in his Sainsbury Building at Worcester College.[3] The courts were sunk slightly below ground level, and above them were six sets of rooms with the bedrooms in east-facing sleeping galleries. The completion of the Garden Quadrangle, immediately to the east, in 1994 supplied more housing for graduate students, as well as undergraduates, in college, and in 1997, with graduate students now numbering 164, the college decided to turn the residential sets over the squash courts into a new Middle Common Room, containing a large 'social space', a television room, two quiet rooms, and a computer room. The former Middle Common Room accommodation on the ground floor of the Sir Thomas White building was now freed for use as meeting and seminar rooms.

The architects chosen for the project were a local firm, Berman, Guedes and Stretton, who had come to prominence with the redevelopment of the site of the former printing works at the Oxford University Press, which were closed in 1990. St John's was their first collegiate project, and they have since gone on to do work at Corpus Christi and Rhodes House, as well as the conversion of the eighteenth-century Old Bank in Oxford's High Street into a hotel and the popular Quod Bar

---

[1] B. Harrison (ed), *History of Oxford University: the Twentieth Century*, p. 211.
[2] *College Record* (1961); see p. 45.
[3] See pp. 78–9.

111 The Middle Common Room exterior (Berman, Guedes and Stretton 1997–8) (Chris Andrews)

112 The interior of the Middle Common Room (Chris Andrews)

and Grill.[4] Their Middle Common Room conversion was deftly carried out, with the addition of a balcony and a lightweight steel-framed, glass-walled extension to the west-facing 'social space' that replaced the sitting rooms of the sets on the first floor (Fig. 111); inside, a curved gallery gives access to the smaller rooms created out of the former bedrooms (Fig. 112). With the completion of this unpretentious but ingenious and serviceable building, at a cost of £530,000, the post-graduate students of St John's could at last enjoy premises that reflected their growing importance in the life of the college.

[4] Berman, Guedes and Stretton, 'Seven Projects' (Dec 2003).

Summary of the Main Architectural Projects carried out 1945–2005[1]

The Dolphin Quadrangle, 1947–8

8 sets of rooms, 2 tutors' studies, a lecture room, bathrooms, and changing rooms

Architect	Edward Maufe
Contractors	Benfield & Loxley
Cost	£43,216
Sources	SJCA, Mun. lxxxi. 45 (papers); Mun. lxxxi. 85 (drawings) *Builder*, (14 January 1949), pp. 47–54

Senior Common Room, Lunch and Meeting room, 1953–5

Architect	David Booth of Booth and Ledeboer
Cost	unknown (original estimate £26,500)
Sources	SJCA, Mun. lxxxi. 50 (papers); Mun. lxxxi. 168 (drawings)

The Beehive, 1958–60

30 bed-sitting rooms, one Fellow's set, one tutor's study, a bicycle store.

Architect	Michael Powers of the Architects' Co-Partnership
Contractors	Benfield & Loxley
Cost	£81,700
Sources	SJCA, Mun. lxxxi. 53, 59 (papers); Mun. lxxxi. 235–8 (drawings). There are also some uncatalogued preliminary designs in the Muniment Room *Architects' Journal*, (17 November 1960), pp. 725–34 *Architectural Review*, 128 (September 1960), pp. 104–9

Tutors' Houses, Blackhall Road, 1962–3

2 semi-detached houses and one detached house

Architect	Michael Powers of the Architects' Co-Partnership
Contractors	T. H. Kingerlee & Sons
Cost	£30,214
Sources	SJCA, Mun. lxxxi. 243. *Architects' Journal*, (26 June 1963), pp. 1347–56

[1] Internal alterations to pre-1945 buildings, and building away from the college's main site, are not included.

Sir Thomas White Building, 1972–5

75 bed-sitting rooms, 75 sets, bar, Junior Common Room, Middle Common Room, porter's lodge

Architect	Philip Dowson of Arup Associates
Contractors	Johnson & Bailey
Cost (approximate)	£1,500,000
Sources	SJCA, Mun. lxxxi. 170, 172, 179 (papers); Mun. lxxxi. 94–109, 150–1, 178 (designs and drawings)
	Architectural Review, (December 1977), pp. 357–60
	Arup Journal, (14 April 1979), 2–14

Senior Common Room, Sadler Room , 1980–1

Reception room

Architects	Howard Colvin, and Walter Price of the Oxford Architects Partnership
Cost	£79,000
Sources	SJCA, Mun.lxxxi. 139, 140

The Garden Quadrangle, 1991–4

50 bed-sitting rooms, 4 sets for Junior Research Fellows, auditorium and ancillary facilities, dining/reception room and kitchen, display gallery for historic vestment collection, library storage, music practice rooms.

Architect	Richard MacCormac of MacCormac Jamieson & Pritchard
Structural engineer	Price & Myers
Contractors	Try Construction
Cost (approximate)	£8,500,000
Sources	SJCA, Mun.lxxxi. 230 (papers); files in Bursary; feasibility studies, architects's designs and drawings (in Bursary)
	Architects' Journal, 14 November 1990, 14–17
	Architectural Review, 193 (October 1994), pp. 43–9
	Building, (11 March 1994), pp. 34–8

Middle Common Room, 1997–8

New common room and ancillary facilities above squash courts

Architect	Berman, Guedes and Stretton

Senior Common Room Extension, 2003–4

Lunch room, sitting room, kitchens

Architect	Richard MacCormac of MacCormac, Jamieson, and Pritchard
Structural engineer	Price & Myers

Select Bibliography

Brawne, Michael, *Arup Associates* (London 1983).

[Anthony Cox], *Architects' Co-Partnership: the First 50 Years* (privately published, 1989).

Chablo, Diane, 'University Architecture in Britain 1950–1975', D. Phil. thesis, Oxford University, 1987.

Colvin, Howard, *Unbuilt Oxford* (New Haven and London 1983).

Dictionary of National Biography 1971–1981, entry on Sir Edward Maufe.

Harrison, Brian (ed.), *The History of the University of Oxford*, Vol. VII, *The Twentieth Century* (Oxford 1994).

Hinchcliffe, Taris, *North Oxford* (New Haven and London 1992).

Mabbott, John, *Oxford Memories* (Oxford 1986).

Morgan, A. L. & Naylor, C. (eds), *Contemporary Architects* (Chicago and London 1987).

Muthesius, Stefan, *The Post-War University: Utopianist Campus and College* (New Haven and London 2001).

Reed, D., and Opher, Philip, *New Architecture in Oxford* (Oxford 1977).

St John's College Record (from 1986 *St John's College Notes*) (Oxford, published annually).

Sillery, A. & V., *St John's College Biographical Register 1919–1975* (Oxford: St John's College, 1978).

Stevens, Robert, *University to Uni* (London 2004).

Taylor, Nicholas and Booth, Philip, *Cambridge New Architecture* (London 1970).

Tyack, Geoffrey, *Oxford: an Architectural Guide* (Oxford 1980).

Tyack, Geoffrey, *St John's College: a Short History and Guide* (Oxford: St John's College, 2000).

www.mjparchitects.co.uk (website of MacCormac, Jamieson, and Pritchard).

Photographic Credits

Chris Andrews: *Frontispiece, Figs. 8, 9, 24, 27, 54, 62, 63, 64, 67, 68, 73, 80, 93, 94, 103, 104, 106, 111, 112*

Architects' Co-Partnership: *Figs. 11, 15, 16, 17, 21, 22, 23, 25, 26, 29, 31, 32, 33, 37, 108*

Architects' Journal: Fig. 34

Arup Associates: *Figs. 47, 50, 51, 52, 55, 56, 57, 60, 61*

Ashmolean Museum, Oxford: *Fig. 85*

Julian Bicknell: *Fig. 69*

Bodleian Library, University of Oxford: *Fig. 2*

Cambridge 2000: *Figs. 21, 49*

Corbis Inc.: *Fig. 53*

Sir Philip Dowson: *Fig. 35*

English Heritage, National Monuments Record: *Figs. 74, 77*

John Howard: *Fig. 82*

MacCormac, Jamieson and Prichard: *Figs. 72, 83, 86, 88, 90, 91, 92, 95–101*

Robert Maguire: *Fig. 70*

Oxford University Press: *Fig . 84*

Oxfordshire County Council Photographic Archive: *Figs. 5, 6, 36*

Alan Powers: *Fig. 13*

RIBA Library Photographic Collection: *Fig. 48*

Saunders Boston Ltd: *Fig 71*

The trustees of Sir John Soane's Museum: *Fig. 87*

The Twentieth Century Society: *Fig. 14*

Geoffrey Tyack: *Figs 19, 20, 107*

All other illustrations are reproduced by permission of the President and Fellows of St John's College and, where relevant, the architects.

Index

References to illustrations are italicised. The principal references to buildings discussed in the text are in bold. Buildings in colleges, including St John's, are listed under the college.